P9-CTP-018

Jo, C. G.

thinking

E DUE

Rethinking How We Age

Recent Titles in Contributions in Philosophy

Rethinking DISCARDED
How
We Age

A New View of
The Aging Mind

C. G. PRADO

Contributions in Philosophy, Number 28

Greenwood Press
Westport, Connecticut • London, England

Library of Congress Cataloging in Publication Data

Prado, C. G.
  Rethinking how we age.

  (Contributions in philosophy, ISSN 0084–926X ; no. 28)
  Bibliography: p.
  Includes index.
    1. Aging—Psychological aspects. 2. Aged—Attitudes.
3. Self-perception. 4. Aged—Public opinion. 5. Aging—
Social aspects. I. Title. II. Series.
  BF724.55.A35P73 1986   155.67   85–9862
  ISBN 0–313–24785–4 (lib. bdg. : alk. paper)

Library of Congress Catalog Card Number: 85–9862
ISBN: 0–313–24785–4
ISSN: 0084–926X

First published in 1986

Greenwood Press
A division of Congressional Information Service, Inc.
88 Post Road West
Westport, Connecticut 06881

Printed in the United States of America

∞

The paper used in this book complies with the
Permanent Paper Standard issued by the National
Information Standards Organization (Z39.48–1984).

10 9 8 7 6 5 4 3 2 1

For Concha,
and for Martyn

Contents

Preface

This book is about perspective change. It is also about aging. It is about both because, whether we realize it or not, expectations about, and the reality of, perspective change as we age constitute central parts of how our lives progress. The book is addressed to rather diverse groups of people. It is addressed to those who feel that something more synoptic is needed beyond the great abundance of data we have on aging. It is addressed to those who feel that our present attitudes toward aging and the aged are unfortunate and need to be revised, if only because of the increasing proportion of older people. The book is also addressed to those who find perspective changes intriguing, whether in the old or the young. And it is addressed to those who are open to new proposals for their own sake.

The groups described are not easily delineable in terms of professions or other easy "target" descriptions. I am not, for instance, addressing gerontologists or philosophers as such. This makes the book somewhat anomalous, given our contemporary craving for categorization. However, I hope that my proposal to change how we think about perspective change in aging, and hence about aging and the aged, will be considered in spite of its lack of specific disciplinary legitimation.

My proposal is essentially an attempt to reintroduce a measure of mythopoeic thinking into how we construe the intellectual or conceptual changes that seem to accompany aging. The point is to complement the mass of theory and the even greater mass of data we have on growing old with something more personally socially productive.

Dealing with the old and growing old involve intimately personal aspects that must fall through the net of theory because of theory's inherent generality. My concern is with some of those aspects, especially how individuals see other individuals significantly older than themselves and how they see themselves as they age. But I need to provide some theory as a backdrop to my general proposal. The reason is that while the proposal is one about our attitudes, it rests on a more fundamental proposal about conceptualization and the role of narrative in conceptualization. I also need to provide some practical ideas, as a way of indicating the force and advantages of my proposal. One way to describe the resulting complexity is to say that my proposal is in "applied" philosophy. A less happy description is that I must make compromises in both the conceptual and empirical areas. But there must still be room for discussions such as the one that follows. The alternative is to restrict ourselves to established disciplines and areas, to existing vocabularies and topics. I think perspective change in aging is a topic that is important enough in our lives to merit open discussion unhindered by a priori disciplinary and terminological distinctions. And I think it important enough to merit a generous measure of patience on the part of participants in discussion. Therefore, I invite the reader to approach what follows in a mood of intellectual and disciplinary ecumenism.

In the chapters that follow I shall be concerned with what are now distinguished as *psychological* and *social* age, in contrast to *biological* age. Both of the former have to do with roles and perceptions, as opposed to the state of one's body. I shall, however, often be concerned with *chronological* age, precisely because sheer chronological age is so often of lesser importance than our expectations and prejudices allow.[1]

Malcolm Cowley says of psychological and social age that "we start by growing old in other people's eyes, then slowly we come to share their judgment."[2] Psychological age is construed mainly in terms of adaptive capacities, and social age largely in terms of the parts we play as a result of how we see ourselves and how others see us. My central concern will be with assumptions of diminished adaptive capacity and the relation of those assumptions to self-perception and perception by others. My objective is to propose a more productive way of thinking and speaking about the changes that do occur or that we take to occur in adaptive capacity as we age.

The problem I am addressing is a general and diffuse presumption that equates advanced aging with decreasing adaptive capacity or narrowing of perspectives. The presumption is most likely a hangover from earlier times when living past one's fifties was a rare and very mixed blessing. Attitudes perhaps apropriate to those times have survived in our ways of speaking about aging and hence in our ways of thinking about aging. But medical and technological advances have dealt with the grosser problems of old age, and better nutrition, education, and so on have made earlier attitudes obsolete. We now face the need to appreciate fully the way our culture is changing and has changed with the proportional increase in older members. But we must also change certain attitudes in order to make conceptual room for those older members as full-fledged participants in culture.

In the chapters that follow I shall outline a proposal that may go some way toward changing outdated attitudes. The point is to knock down confining attitudinal walls, to change how we think about aging. We need a new conceptual matrix; especially we need a new of thinking about how perspectives change as we age. Heideggerian "new words" must be spoken. It is not enough to continue amassing data on aging and hoping that its sheer bulk will alter basic attitudes. Age undoubtably brings changes, but it does not make us different by making us *less* as a consequence of years lived.

My aim is to suggest how certain changes that seem real enough in aging are better thought of as functions of what we *do* than of what we *become*. The need for the proposal is that we must come fully to grips with a form of life that now includes many more whose perspectives on that form of life have been shaped by much more extensive participation in it than ever before.

Rethinking
How
We Age

1

Introduction

Conception of the aged as a homogeneous group marked by above-average dependency on others, special economic needs, health problems, and a general decline of competency and productivity is too often characteristic both of the common view of the aged and of more expert interest in the aged and aging. The elderly are seen as are the handicapped, as a group posing problems because of certain intrinsic characteristics. As a group the aged are contrasted with the "responsible adults" of the late twenties through early fifties range who are deemed the norm in our society, a status gained, incidentally, in part by the classification of human beings as "teenagers" and "senior citizens" at either end of the spectrum.

The lumping of the elderly into a problematic group is a methodological necessity for the various groups and institutions concerned with them, for these could not function if they addressed themselves to individuals. But the result is that individual elderly people then tend to be perceived in a way that characterizes them in terms of the properties attributed to the statistical group. The negative general view of the elderly is thereby "legitimized". It then becomes necessary to treat particular elderly people as exceptional in certain respects, in and out of institutions. Special ascriptions are used: "She's seventy-two but sharp as a tack." "He's nearly eighty but still productive." What is needed is simple recognition of individual elderly people as they are.

Conception of the elderly as a special group characterized by deficiencies results in the perception of individual old people first as problematic in some way and only secondarily as competent. Against this, a thirty-year-old is perceived first as competent and only secondarily as problematic in terms of some special condition, for example, a drinking problem or a physical handicap. The consequence is in effect the creation of a new minority in the sense of a group vulnerable to prejudice. If aging were simply a matter of universal and consistent mental and physical deterioration, perception of the elderly as generally deficient would be justified. But a great many elderly individuals are simply competent adults. It is true that they share special problems as a statistical group, but so do adolescents and the middle-aged. An obsession with being popular or a pervasive conviction of failure can be as debilitating as arthritis or increasing forgetfulness. Reasonably resourceful people can cope with any of these. The problems of the elderly are most often just different, as opposed to being somehow of a piece in a way that amounts to a lessening of the individuals who bear them.[1]

Neutral perception of individual elderly people as only chronologically older is readily precluded by perhaps the most pervasive negative attitude toward the elderly, which has to do with expectations about their adaptive capacity and perspectives. Expressions like "You can't teach an old dog new tricks" signal a widespread view that the elderly are set in their ways, that they find it difficult to adapt to new circumstances or to learn new techniques. This view may be based on some experience with particular elderly individuals on the part of persons holding it, but it is a view that is immediately generalized in a broad and persistent way. Even if an elderly person is taken to be free of physical deficiencies, he or she will be suspect to a significantly younger person because of assumed problematic perception and orientation, dubious priorities, questionable values, and/or lack of interest and awareness. The ready assumption of senility is largely not based on assumption of specific disorders. In fact, many people are unaware of the fact that there are various sorts of senility and that each involves particular underlying physical conditions. There is an exaggerated readiness to see symptoms of incompetence in those of advanced age, whether or not that incompetence is deemed to have physical causes. As a forty-six-year-old academic my forgetfulness is taken as a badge of office and as no bar to abstract thought. If I were sixty-six or seventy, it would be perceived very differently, whether or not it was assumed to relate to some persisting organic condition. It would be taken as confirming incompetence due to age as such, as opposed to, say, specially focused interests.

Studies do show that the elderly tend to retain less in short-term memory and that their reaction times, in both the mental and physical areas of task performance, are somewhat slower.[2] But once we allow for educational differences, motivation, and so on, there is at least no clear reason to believe that intellectual competence deteriorates on a par with physical competence or simply with the passing of time. Yet a common perception of the elderly is one that assumes intellectual deterioration as a necessary accompaniment of chronological age.

Sociologists and psychologists are, of course, eager to understand the hows and whys of our perception and treatment of the elderly. But there is a need for a philosophical contribution to our views on aging. In particular there is need to say something about the presumption of intellectual deterioration. We need a way of considering possible perspective change of an unfortunate sort, a way that detaches that change from aging as such, so that we may better understand where we are right and where we are wrong in taking the very weight of years to be intellectually debilitating.

Many of our present attitudes toward the elderly clearly incorporate a presumption of perspective narrowness or inflexibility. And there is reason to suspect that the reality does not support this presumption, that the elderly are not a homogeneous group with respect to perspective or other mental deficiencies.[3] I do not want to suggest that there is no mental change accompanying physical aging. I am not, for instance, a dualist willing to divorce "the mind" from an ever more worn body. But I do think that we need a new way of speaking about the changes that may take place, a way that does not prejudice us against the aged generally by yoking one or another sort of mental or perspective deterioration with sheer chronological aging. We all grow old, but perhaps we do not all deteriorate intellectually as we do. It is also important to learn to speak about such changes that may occur in ways that do not encourage or predispose the young to acquire negative expectations about their abilities as they grow older.

A new way of speaking about perspective change in aging has certain clear requirements. First, it must not isolate individuals of a given age range as somehow generally problematic in terms of presumptions of incompetence. But neither should it mask the realities of special difficulties. In dealing with the handicapped, for instance, the point is to do so in a way that acknowledges their special requirements without lessening them as persons in doing so and especially without promoting generalizations from their special difficulties to other aspects of their personalities.

A second requirement is that we be able to describe perspective changes in aging as natural developments rather than as unnatural in the sense of being pathological. Aging is not an unnatural process. The parallel here is to the way pregnancy is perversely considered by some doctors as a malady. There is admittedly some physical deterioration in aging, but we are rather special creatures, and there is another aspect to aging as self-conscious, rational beings: namely, participation in a form of life over a great many years. This aspect has its own consequences, and the negative ones should not be automatically attributed to or identified with physical deterioration or, perhaps worse, seen to be an inevitable, though mysterious, consequence of growing older.

What present ways of dealing with perspective change in aging do not allow is the amassing of experience over a great many years without connotations of entailed growing deficiency. Even when we go to the very old for special reasons, to see what it is like to have spanned the steam and atomic ages or to remember the Civil War, we do so condescendingly, allowing, as we feel we must, for narrowed perspectives and naiveté concerning present developments. Quite simply, we patronize the very old as we patronize the very young. We deem both less than our intellectual equals. And it is significant that when the old deal with the young, they willingly adopt the role of child for the sake of utility. An old man will play on his nurse's expectations to get what he wants, just as a child soon learns to do.

The preceding raises the very real question of whether the young and the middle-aged understand the aged. If we ask this question with respect to adolescents from the perspective of middle age we do so in a rhetorical way and never fully seriously. However baffled we are by adolescent attitudes, we are mindful of two things: We were once adolescents ourselves, and adolescents will soon be like us. Our juxtaposition to the elderly is very different. While we may soon be like them, we have never been elderly. A new way of speaking about perspective change in aging must allow for and encourage great interpretive latitude. The discourse of the aged requires special interpretation. Our tendency is to hear what is said by an elderly person as somehow simpler, due to a paring away of inessentials or to narrower perspectives or to obsessive concerns, such as with health. But we should realize that what we are hearing is a function of very significantly greater lived experience. What we hear requires special attention and not a little postulation. This is perhaps the heart of the matter: We must understand that what the aged say presupposes much that is not open to us. This is not to say that the mere piling up of experience necessarily results in greater complexity or depth. This is a point about background required for understanding, not about evaluation. Ronald Blythe provides a perceptive example:

> The most irreconcilable aspect of age is the destruction of progressive movement, that hard fact of having come to the end ... when custom and instinct still insist that one can and should go on. ... When the old say ... "I simply can't go on," they are stating their major frustration, not announcing a coming to terms with death.[4]

"I can't go on" is not an admission of acquiescence or of despair. But it can be understood as an acknowledgement and as a statement against blind expectation only if one factors in certain realizations and a great weight of experience.

A new way of speaking about perspective change in aging, then, requires at least avoidance of isolating elderly individuals in some invidious way, treatment of the process of aging and some of the changes it brings as natural as opposed to pathological, and, perhaps most important, awareness of the need for consciously perspicuous and generous interpretation of what is said to us by those significantly older than ourselves. This latter point is a tricky one, for it is just here that we sell the elderly short. We tend not so much to interpret, carefully and sympathetically, but to impose our expectations on what we hear. It would be an ambitious and likely pretentious undertaking to attempt the production of a new vocabulary with respect to so extensive an aspect of our form of life as perspective change in aging. A more manageable project is the proposal of a scheme to facilitate production of such a vocabulary. And the latter proposal can be made in the context of discussing something very puzzling, namely, why, at least in our culture, we think of age as *narrowing* instead of broadening. In many cultures the aged are valued for their wisdom and breadth. It may be speculation, but it seems that in our technologically oriented culture we tend to think of the aged as becoming obsolete along with the gadgetry of their generation. But whatever the underlying reasons, much of the negative attitude toward the elderly has to do with thinking them less flexible, narrower in their interests, less able to deal with new ideas and situations. This attitude is evident enough in what people say, but it is also evident in the abundance of studies concerned to show that, say, creativity does not necessarily decrease as one ages.[5] Such studies are often undertaken and presented as counters to widespread opinions.

I think that the perspective narrowing we so readily assume is sometimes real enough, but I think it is best understood not in terms of growing old or the piling up of experience, but rather in terms of the consequences of how we deal with experience. To make this out I shall contend that perspective narrowing is a result of how we shape and define experience. Much of what follows will be given over to making out this proposal, but here I can begin by articulating a kind of basic principle: Given the creatures we are, given the nature of our thought and awareness, it seems that broadness of perspective is of fundamental importance to us. To flourish as human beings certainly must be to broaden our perspectives. We count breadth of vision precisely as the main mark of maturity (and perversely deny such maturity to the oldest among us). Anything that restricts us, from obsession to mental or physical impediments to simple ignorance, must be bad. Perspective breadth can be viewed otherwise only from some single restrictive perspective, such as a defensive religious or political one.

It would seem that as we grow older, our perspective horizon should widen if for no other reason than the range of experience. But our negative presumption of perspective narrowness in the aged runs counter to this expectation. And the dominance of this negative view indicates that it does have some basis. What I want to suggest is that there is something I shall dub "interpretive parsimony". This is little more than stereotypic thinking, reliance on favoured metaphors and constructions, and the tendency to respond to new situations in ways we have responded to old ones. But we need a way to pull these things together, to be able to speak of them as parts of a single process by which perspectives narrow. Perhaps the reliance on favoured and even compulsive metaphors is the key point.[6] The central idea is that too many of us too often respond to the world in "tried and true" ways rather than make use of other options. But doing so has nothing to do with aging as such. It has to do with what I want to insist is actually training in interpretive parsimony. The trouble is that we automatically attribute to the elderly something like extreme interpretive parsimony, and we probably do so mainly by projection of continually increasing tendencies in ourselves. But recognition of these tendencies in ourselves is invariably of a rationalized sort. We think ourselves growing more knowledgeable and sophisticated, less gullible. We misperceive increasing narrowness as growing competence. It is others who grow inflexible.

At some time interpretive parsimony was probably a survival factor. The inclination to make do with few constructions of the contents of experience no doubt increased the biological fitness of creatures operating in a fairly stable environment. The alternative would be an inclination to unbridled imaginativeness and would actually be detrimental to problem solving. Dogged determination often serves us better than creativity. A population would seem to need very few inventive geniuses to provide novel ideas and new ways of looking at things. In the case of individuals, interpretive parsimony is necessary, as well as productive, because of the need to order experience into bases for action. Without such ordering the individual could not behave in a manner relevant to his or her environment.

But what interests me is that, whatever our theories about underlying mechanisms, an increase of experience does not appear to produce perspective breadth often enough to counter general presumption of increasing narrowness. I am suggesting that the likeliest reason is that in a sense experience does not really increase, because our organizing and structuring of new experience gerrymander it into familiar shapes. What we see in persons who are interpretively parsimonious to excess, then, is the fruit not of broad and serially extensive experience at all, but rather of inhibitory practices. The sheer amount of experience is actually irrelevant. The pail of an individual's intellectual capacity can carry only so much water, regardless of how much may be poured over it. And I am proposing that some of the limitations of that capacity are due to acquired interpretive habits that are initially productive but can become counterproductive.

I am arguing that increase of interpretive parsimony is related to aging only in that we grow older in the process of having more experience. Yet interpretive parsimony, to the extent that it is recognized, seems to be attributed to the elderly simply on the basis of growing older. An accompanying characteristic is being taken to be a consequence of aging. What we need to do is to find how to discuss interpretive parsimony in a way that satisfies the requirements I outlined for a new way of speaking about perspective change in aging. I want to suggest that the reason for an increase of interpretive parsimony beyond need is success. That is, we do seem to manage with a small number of interpretive structures and techniques, so experience seems not to broaden us as much as confirm us in our procedures. For one thing, we are usually discouraged from being innovative. The truth of this is perhaps best illustrated by the way that groups tend to reinforce practices and prejudices rather than challenge them. Beyond this, so much of our life is structured or "scripted", for instance by experts who take us through child rearing and who detail the complexities of our midlife crises. We are constantly exposed to advertising that relies on fostering stereotypic thinking and the acceptance of invented types carrying normative implications ("the Marlboro man", "the Pepsi generation"). The media contributes by structuring the news in terms of types ("supply-siders", "single-issue advocates"). In our culture we can think narrowly without danger. There is little premium put on working ourselves out of interpretive parsimony. In fact, a good deal of therapy in our culture has to consist of getting people to abandon certain stereotypes of themselves. We are in effect trained to be interpretively parsimonious, at least in being provided with most of the few interpretive structures we do use and being encouraged by peer pressure to conform to certain interpretive practices. This is evident in the very area with which we are concerned, aging. The application of expertise has resulted not only in the demarcation of a special class, as noted earlier, but really in something like a "definition" of aging. We now have a discipline, gerontology, within which thirty-year-olds can believe they understand the essence of growing and being old. Aging has been circumscribed and problematic perceptions of it institutionalized.[7] Jonathan Swift somewhere said that there is "no world" for an old man. The trouble now seems to be that the only room allowed for the old has been conceptually delineated by the young. And in the process of delineation the young are taught how to be old. The advantage of speaking of perspective change in the way I shall describe is that we shall then be able to deal with perspective narrowing in terms of inhibitory practices rather than in terms of the consequences of deterioration or the mere passage of time. Discussing perspective change in aging in terms of narrative employment will allow considering perspective narrowing in a way that does not isolate older people in an invidious way. Perspective narrowing will be construed not as deterioration but as an undesirable by-product of how we process experience.

The proposed way of speaking is mainly intended to make us more aware of the fact that perspective narrowing, when it occurs, is not a function of aging as such. And it will help us realize that our presumption of deteriorative narrowing in the elderly is itself a matter of interpretive parsimony.

My proposal will also meet the other requirements mentioned. It will allow description of perspective narrowing as a natural phenomenon rather than a pathological one. I am not, of course, discounting psychological and physical factors, only proposing that actual pathological difficulties be considered realistically, namely, as exceptional. I want to describe a process that no single psychological or physical deficiency or set of related psychological and physical deficiencies explains. I want to show that perspective narrowing is a consequence of how we think, not a matter of coming to think less well, or just less, because of hardening of the arteries or a growing paucity of brain cells. Undoubtably I shall have to relate my conclusions to such deficiencies, but the point is that we need a better, more comprehensive account of perspective changes than could be available in terms of physical deficiencies. We find too many twenty-year-olds and eighty-year-olds failing to conform to expected patterns to attribute parsimony confidently to physical changes.

But perhaps most important is the fact that my proposal will meet the requirement of interpretive latitude. If we understand that perspective narrowing may be due to parsimonious practices, and not necessarily to deterioration, we can attend to at least some of the utterances of the elderly as we do to texts. We can employ a hermeneutic approach in trying to understand what can be meant in light of different historical backgrounds. That is, we can attend to what significantly older people say to us while mindful of our biases and what Hans-Georg Gadamer calls "prejudgments". We can be alert to diversity of historical background and take deliberate care in how we construe what is said. Rather than presuming incompetence of one sort or another, we can acknowledge crucial experiential diversity and its consequent influence on what is said to us by those older than ourselves.

I do not want to enter here into an extended discussion of

hermeneutics or, very broadly, theories of interpretation. All I need is the idea that understanding what the elderly say to us, at least in some contexts, requires interpretation of a special order. The difficulties of understanding that we face are comparable to those concerning historicity in understanding texts of significantly earlier periods. Though elderly individuals are obviously contemporaries of ours, in one sense their utterances (again, in some contexts) have a different historical base, one as closed to us as any more temporally distant one.

The general hermeneutical problem is one of understanding how meaning is "recognized as such by a subject and transposed into his own system of values and meanings".[8] In the case of the elderly we have the special problem of what might be described as a significant, though clearly not total, disparity of historical "place". A thirty-year-old speaking to a sixty-year-old is dealing with someone whose experience encompasses what can only be history to the former. The problem of one person's understanding another is complicated by the fact that one of those persons inhabits a world that differs not only with respect to personal perspective, but also with respect to what it encompasses as "actual". Even though long past, some events will be constitutive elements of the sixty-year-old's awareness, but they can only be information to the thirty-year-old.

It is important to be clear on what my objective is. Proposing a new way of speaking and thinking about perspective narrowing and aging is not a matter of addressing a discerned problem and offering a solution. That would be to deal with a technical problem. The matter is rather different. It is really a question of a creative proposal, a proposal prompted not by discernment of a particular problem, but rather by a conviction that things would be better if the elderly among us, who are growing in numbers, were more often participants in our conversations and stories and less often the subjects of those conversations and stories. My proposal is an attempt to provide a unifying scheme and a key explanatory concept for our present views on how perspectives seem to narrow in aging. And I think that such narrowing or the expectation of it is the root of negative attitudes toward the elderly. There seems to be no clear competitor to assumed or actual perspective narrowing as the most pervasive determinant of how the elderly are seen. This is the other side of the coin to the assumption I am making that perspective breadth is a fundamental value for creatures such as ourselves. And this is a point I cannot seriously question.

Some of the discussion that follows will be rather technical. My proposal about what underlies the way we deal with experience must be made out carefully, precisely because of its simplicity. The proposal about narrative employment is intended to provide a conceptual basis for what I want to say about perspective change in aging. But I must make clear that it is a proposal made in a pragmatic mood. I shall pursue the reasons for using the pragmatic mood below. At this point mention of pragmatism is intended only to signal that I am not setting out to outline a new theory. What I offer is only a way of construing much that is already available to us in psychology and other sciences and would-be sciences, as well as in our present practices. Once narrative employment has been clarified, we will see how that employment can be construed as resulting in perspective narrowing through growing inflexibility and so how it explains interpretive parsimony.

Before proceeding to outline the proposal about narrative employment in the next chapter, I must consider briefly a number of points that might otherwise give rise to confusion.

First, when I speak of broadness of perspective as a fundamental value, am I relying on cognitive adequacy? That is, am I committed to something beyond pragmatism in the sense of construing perspective breadth in terms of greater awareness of truth, or what is the case? This point raises nothing less than the issue between the pragmatist and the adherents of the correspondence theory of truth. In chapter 2 I shall consider this matter, but here I must say at least this: When we are concerned with perspective breadth and interpretive flexibility, we are concerned with more than "what is the case", even assuming that we allow that there is something that "is the case". We are concerned with more than "what is the case" for we are concerned with what is *taken* to be the case or as possibly being the case. My interest is in human perceptions, in construals, not in some putative determinate reality. Human relations and concerns are not tidy enough to "be the case", even if we countenance some sort of rigid realism. A colleague responded to my views once by saying that what is important is discerning "how things really are" for the elderly. But what could that be? And how could anyone tell?

Something else to be noted is that when I spoke above of the need for hermeneutical interpretation of what the elderly say to us, I did not intend to say that hermeneutical interpretation is a special kind of interpretation. My point is that we must interpret what the elderly say in a way that acknowledges the "hermeneutical circle", that is, the roles of anticipation and of postulation that make possible understanding of what presents itself to us, while allowing what presents itself to us to shape understanding. Speaking of understanding texts in terms of oral interpretation, Richard Palmer speaks of the hermeneutical circle in this way:

The process is a . . . paradox: in order to read it is necessary to understand . . . what will be said, and yet this understanding must come from the reading. What begins to emerge . . . is the complex dialectical process involved in all understanding as it grasps the meaning of a sentence, and somehow in a reverse direction supplies the attitude and emphasis which alone can make the written word meaningful.[9]

What the aged say to us, orally or in print, requires that we work at supplying and filling out contexts. As noted above, "I simply can't go on" might be heard as acquiescence or despair, until we think a bit about the perspective from which it is said, until we recall books such as Blythe's or Cowley's and it occurs to us that we are hearing the phrase as if it came from ourselves projected in time. But it comes from someone very different, someone who has lived with what Blythe called the main frustration of the old, the realization that life is all but over, yoked to a yearning to go on. We must stretch our minds to hear the phrase as coming from a point at which the attitude toward death is different, a point at which there is recognition of competing instincts both to acknowledge an end and to continue.

But perhaps enough has been said to launch my project. In what follows I shall attempt first to sketch my proposal about narrative employment and then to say something about its pragmatic cast. After that I shall try to make out more clearly the notion of interpretive parsimony and how it relates to aging. Beyond that the objective will be to try to understand much of what we say about perspective change in aging in terms of the proposal about narrative employment.

The overall thrust of what follows is to show the advantages of a certain model or scheme with respect to thinking and talking about perspective change in aging. Once we use the model proposed, we should realize that perspective narrowing is only incidentally related to aging, or at least that we may more profitably so treat it and speak of it. We should then begin to see that our main basis for isolating the elderly is simply misconceived or at least insufficient. The consequence should be an altered attitude. The change should consist in part of coming to see certain difficulties the elderly must deal with as impairments due to certain practices and not as intrinsic properties of their age group. If we smear grease on our glasses, put pebbles in our shoes, and stuff cotton in our ears, we should appreciate that such handicaps do not lessen us as persons, that such handicaps do not immediately render us more fit to be discoursed about than discoursed with. In like manner, if we understand interpretive parsimony, we should have the same insight regarding the intellectual aspect of growing old.

When we meet noted members of our professions or disciplines who happen to speak another language, we do not think them less. We strive to communicate with a peer in spite of inhibiting factors. When we encounter an old man or woman, why should we not do the same? I think it is because we presume perspective narrowing of an extreme sort, of a sort that importantly precludes significant rapport and productive interaction. If we come to see how and why perspectives do narrow, and how and why and when we may be right to anticipate such narrowness, we should begin to see most people considerably older than ourselves as just that: so many more people with individual traits and problems. We should stop seeing the aged as members of a class jointly excluded from our conversations by perspectives narrowed as a consequence of just growing older.

2

The Shaping of Experience

Interpretive parsimony begins with practical success, and it goes wrong when continued success with familiar ways of interpreting experience renders us blind to new possibilities. But we must resist the temptation to think of it as going wrong in causal terms, because of physical deterioration or the mere piling up of years. The problem is of a different sort; it is one of coming to be insensitive or unresponsive to alternative constructions, of coming to lack facility in diversely juxtaposing certain givens in experience. And this is a lack arising not from obstruction but from success met with in juxtaposing elements in set ways.

But what is it we do so well and come to do too well? Prior to focusing on interpretive parsimony, I must provide a conceptual backdrop that is in effect a proposed construal of conceptualization. Only with this construal in place can parsimony be understood. The construal I want to propose here is that we organize experience narrationally, by the employment of narratives. And I shall further propose that the employment of narratives as organizational and experience-defining devices can become counterproductive, can advance to a point well beyond that to which we must trim and shape experience to cope with it. It is this latter phenomenon that is encountered as evident perspective narrowness.

Narrative is presently the topic of intense discussion in Europe and North America. From Jacques Derrida and Harold Bloom to much lesser lights, many in philosophy and criticism are concerned with the theory of narrative. In this chapter I want to press beyond much of what has been discussed and offer what some will think a radical proposal: namely, that narrative captures how we think, that storytelling is basic to conceptualizing the world and ourselves in any way at all, and that there is a continuum between elemental conceptualization and the stories and accounts we now take as paradigmatic of narrative. We must see that narration is not a special activity we learn, one mode of presentation among others, but is fundamental to how we organize experience.

What we now think of as narration is actually like the development of a practical activity into an art, comparable to the way the utilitarian business of preparing and serving tea was developed by the Japanese into an aesthetically rich ceremony. The common view of narration as a special activity or language game is wrong in suggesting that the activity is a learned one. This is an impression due to how narration has been treated in diverse but limited contexts, that is, as storytelling, reporting, recording, and so on.

We can begin our discussion by recalling the organizational and explanatory work done by what are perhaps the earliest recognized narratives—namely, myths. Myths are crucial to the legitimization of social practices and the explanation of extant conditions. But what is of interest to us is that myths "explain" by providing contexts in which puzzling phenomena are seen as "natural". And what is of special importance is that the contexts in question are provided by narratives. Naturalness is established through the telling of a story.

In discussing myth and the views of Lévi-Strauss, Brian Wicker remarks that by drawing parallels between states of affairs among human beings and among animals of various species, certain myths make "intelligible and tolerable the tensions that exist between different groups within the human community".[1] They do so by making the worrying state of affairs seem the norm through comparison with some state of affairs in another species. A hierarchical structuring in the animal world will be deemed "natural", and a worrying hierarchical structuring among human beings will then be construed as equally natural, in virtue of the parallel drawn. Nothing is explained, in our scientific sense, but because of certain associations something simply ceases to be problematic. Myth shows that at least at certain levels association is effective in spite of the absence of underlying processes. This is a point that is usually overlooked, in that retrospective consideration of myths tends to supply putative causal or other processes as tacitly underlying association. But mythical association does not proceed on the basis of, say, anatomical or functional similarities. It is an invention.

Wicker sees the exhaustiveness of association in mythical explanations as a weakness. This emerges in his discussion of magical explanation. He sees what he calls "sheer contiguity" as devoid of explanatory force, construing proper explanation as the description of underlying process. Speaking of mythical explanations, Wicker remarks that

the actual process whereby the effect is (magically) transferred remains wholly indescribable. This is precisely because it *is* magic: and that means, not that it is a very difficult process to observe or analyze, but simply that it is not a discernible process at all. It is a sheer "contiguity".[2]

Wicker is taking it that mere association is simply juxtaposition; a magical explanation only juxtaposes one event to another. This is the point of "action at a distance". Those who postulate indiscernible processes underlying the magical transformation are really turning magic into an exotic form of causality. Wicker is right about this much: Magic is "sheer contiguity", though the element of volition does play a crucial role with respect to the occasions for magic. That is, volition usually provides the context in which an association is made. There is, of course, no question of the efficacy of such volition, as the matter would arise only if magic actually worked.

However, in talking about association at the level of myth, we are already at a conceptual level at which states of affairs are grasped and may be seen as puzzling or otherwise. My interest is in the efficacy of association at a much more basic level, where what is at stake is precisely taking something as a state of affairs. Myth is useful here, but only as a stepping stone.

Without endorsing theories about a phenomenal "given", we are able to say, in a Kantian mood, that there must be a pre-conceptual "sensuous manifold" that is the stuff of conceptualized awareness.[3] This manifold can never be an object of awareness because the objects of awareness are always features of the manifold conceptualized as objects of one sort or another. The features of the manifold are the raw matter of awareness. What we are aware of is that matter conceptualized as so many particulars. It follows that we might be left with a collection of minimally conceptualized particulars which, if not a Jamesian "blooming, buzzing confusion", would be an insufficient ground for thought, action, or reflection. What is needed is what Kant sought to provide: organization. Hume tried to make do with association but could not quite make it work.

But suppose the putative inadequacy of association as an organizational mechanism at the level of elemental awareness, and also at the level of myth, is due not to an inherent insufficiency but to a misconception? Suppose unease at not discerning underlying principles or processes is due to the wrongheaded expectation that association is here an explanatory device? What if we say that association is achieved at the level of elemental awareness in a way that follows no principles, that the organization it results in is initially and intrinsically arbitrary? Associations at the level in question may be selective devices purely in virtue of simple inclusion and exclusion of the particulars in a minimally objectified sensuous manifold; inclusion and exclusion may follow no principles, and may not be governed by cognitive processes, though this is not to say association is not determined by causal factors in "the order of being".

The alternative to association that is ungoverned is either to postulate causal processes of a cognitive nature that explain association or to make it intentional. In the former case we are in fact changing the subject to theorizing about basic psychology; in the latter case we are either initiating an infinite regress or simply precluding elemental association. All we actually need to do is postulate an indefinite number of incipient associational combinations of the particulars in awareness, presented to cognition as combinations, and some selection process. What constitutes the "combinations" is phenomenological prominence of some items and relative phenomenological recession of others. The explanation of such prominence and recession is a matter for psychology and neurophysiology. What concerns us is that these combinations constitute stimuli. The selection process, what then "fixes" some, what makes them objects of awareness as combinations or sequences, is inchoate or actual action. Given action, it is productiveness, or possibly impressive failure, that preserves certain associational combinations beyond the point of being stimuli so that they become objects of reflection as integrated sequences.

The suggestion, then, is that just as we may speak of a level at which there is a preconceptual sensuous manifold and a level at which there is minimal objectification, we may speak of a level at which there is initial organization of the objectified particulars. But that organization does not proceed by intentional selection. Part of the point of my proposal is that the fundamental bases for action are experiential sequences that are products of sentience and, as we shall see, imagination but not products of cognitive activity. That is, they are not perceptions in the sense of involving judgement and focused or deliberate attention. Such perceptions come later. It is important that there not be cognitive principles or processes at work in this elemental selection. Once there are sequences of objectified particulars, some will prove productive in supporting action and/or become part of more elaborate sequences and hence will survive as sequences for reflective awareness. The majority will be minutely short-lived. In this sense the proposal is Darwinian, in that selection proceeds without intentional guidance.

I must note here that when I say "we may speak" I mean just that. I take myself to be offering a pragmatic proposal, to be suggesting a useful vocabulary, not attempting to describe how things "really" proceed. Nonetheless, the realists among us may prefer to think of the productivity of some associational sequences being due to their coinciding with how things "really are". My own preference is to take the pragmatic stance. One important advantage of that stance is that it may be left to complementary theories to give an account of the nature of the elements in organizational narratives.

We are a now long way from Wicker's magical explanations, but not so far from the point that for some purposes "sheer contiguity" is sufficient, if not as explanation, then as an organizational device. But what I want to propose now is that the above associational sequences are best described as narrational in nature.

I shall begin to make out how elemental associational sequences are narratives by appealing to cognitive science. The heart of such science is the view that we think by constructing and manipulating internal representations of the world, that we form "hypotheses" in a "language of thought", though these hypotheses need not be propositional.[4] In fact, cognitive psychologists have revived images to serve where propositional content or what Peter Geach would call "saying in one's heart" is insufficient or inappropriate.[5]

The relevance of the cognitive thesis is that associational sequences construed as narratives seem ideally suited to explaining how we form and manipulate "internal representations". These internal representations are elemental in constituting how the world is for someone. Wicker makes a related point about elementalness with respect to some narratives: "The story does not *contain* the answer, it *is* the answer. The answer cannot be translated into factual . . . form, for the answer *is* the narrative form."[6]

What Wicker is bringing out is that where there is no underlying process to describe, the narrative form simply is the "presentation" of a situation. We cannot separate form from content, for the narrative form, in structuring an event, is itself the content in the sense that the event is identical with that structure. At a low enough level a story does not recapitulate anything outside itself. Where events are independently structured—say, by other stories—a narrative can recapitulate a separate content.

Associational sequences or narratives serve well as basic "representations". But they are not representations at all; they are original bases for action in the sense of themselves constituting what the world is for someone at a given point. Associational sequences are the basic stories that provide us with a world, as more conceptually advanced and self-consciously produced stories provide us with other worlds. The story character of organizational narratives is what makes them bases for action and not mere inventories. We should attribute to ourselves a propensity to weave what we encounter into progressive, integrated stories. Whether genetically or psychologically construed, by attributing this propensity to ourselves, we can make sense of much that is otherwise puzzling. Organizational narratives allow a smooth transition from mere objectification to more complex conceptual activity and to action. They provide us with plausible content for the idea that our bases for action are internal representations or scenarios. They show how initial association does not require guiding principles or cognitive processes we would be hard put to locate. By introducing a propensity to tell stories, we also make some sense of how these elemental organizational sequences are not mere inventories. But this raises the problem that the propensity looks too ad hoc. I must make out the idea somewhat more carefully.

The propensity to organize experience narrationally seems an alternative to more direct association, such as in terms of the colors of features of awareness, or distance from us, or some such. Central to narrational association is the way items in a sequence or narrative are construed as responsible for other items. It is as if a "program" is at work, arbitrarily fitting whatever comes along in experience into a set structure, sometimes with productive results, sometimes with neutral or disastrous results. A narrative, at this level, is basically a developmental presentation, and as such a narrative is the sole way we have of conceptualizing a series of events as events and then as occurring or as having occurred or as projected.

As constitutive of a sequence of events, a basic organizational narrative just is how things are for someone. And this involves something common to narratives and more familiar stories: namely, progressiveness. But this is very difficult to articulate. The idea of a narrative seems too basic. "Narrative" is defined in dictionaries in terms of the recounting of a sequence of events.

But it is precisely what makes a sequence of events an integrated narrative that is passed over. Nor can we speak here of causal connection, for it is precisely causal connection that we are in part trying to understand, namely, what it is to see one event as bringing about another. I want to contend that what it is to see the world as causally interconnected, what it is to see a world as opposed to chaos, begins with presentation in organizational narrative.

Incidentally, I am not yet concerned with the distinction between "factual" and "fictional" narratives. First of all, this is a distinction I want to challenge to some extent; second, the organizational sequences I am calling narratives will include items from both perception and imagination. Even Wicker accepts the standard view that fiction is "any story that tells of something that has not in fact happened."[7] But this view cannot apply to a level at which the "story" is a presentation that is how the world is for someone. The point is that elemental stories do not tell of anything at all, in the sense of having a distinct subject matter that is independent of them as narrative structures.

What I am saying, then, is that our associational sequences are narratives in that they constitute presentations of how things are or are taken to be. But to be such, they cannot be mere sequences. They must have a certain integrity and progressiveness, or they must be taken as having these. Otherwise these basic internal presentations would be static or hopelessly jumbled. They could not serve as bases for action.

I am left with the problem of saying what it is that constitutes the progressive, developmental nature of basic narratives. I may be able to avoid postulating operant principles in initial inclusion or association by relying on phenomenological prominence. But inclusion cannot be mere compilation. I must explain how we go so quickly from barely conceptualized material to full-blown narratives, how association blooms immediately into sequences of integrated events. But narrational progressiveness is so basic to our way of thinking that we find it hard to pin down. And because we employ it is, of course, no reason to believe that we understand it.

As noted, dictionary definitions of narrative are of little help.

More literary definitions are not much better: "narrative may be defined simply as the representation of a real or fictional event or series of events by language."[8]

Such definitions go on to distinguish between *diegesis* or narrative and *mimesis* or imitation and also between narrative on the one hand and *description* and *discourse* on the other. Narrative is largely the telling of what happened and as such seems to be downgraded with respect to imitation and to be seen often as only a backdrop for more interesting description and discourse. For instance, it is in description and particularly discourse that fiction is thought to bear its deepest content. The separating out and downgrading of narrative as merely a sort of progressive context goes back to Plato, who saw narration as inferior to imitation, the former being further removed from reality.

But none of the preceding is of any use with respect to understanding narrative integrity. And we might expect that even if there were reference to narrative integrity, beyond the aesthetic, it would still disappoint us as it would bear on the integrity and progressiveness of familiar, full-fledged narratives. This is why current debate on the nature of narrative and on such issues as the "illusion of sequentiality" by figures like Hayden White and Nelson Goodman is of little help to us. These discussions treat narrative as *a* form of presentation. The governing assumptions are referentialist in nature. They cast narrative as always about independent events. Consider White's views. He does insist that "to raise the question of the nature of narrative is to invite reflection on the very nature of culture," but he goes on to say: "So natural is the impulse to narrate, so inevitable is the form of narrative for any report of *the ways things really happened.*"[9] He sees narrative as the solution to the problem of "how to translate *knowing* into *telling*," and he goes further and invokes Roland Barthes to say that narrative is a cross-cultural "meta-code". But he stops short of conceiving of narrative as I want to, as exhaustive and constitutive of experiential order at a low enough level. Goodman also stops short. He explores the flexibility of narrative order or sequentiality, but he finally says that "the general lesson . . . is that while narrative will normally survive all sorts

of contortions, still sometimes when we start with a tale, enough twisting may leave us without one."[10]
But it is precisely starting with a referential tale that we want to avoid. We see here the grip of the referentialist view that the essence of language is the mirroring of the world, that narratives must have subjects. Their integrity, pliable though it may be, is still a function of the progressiveness of something beyond the narrative. Against this I want to construe narratives, at least as organizational sequences, as elemental with respect to order. We need to understand narrative integrity at a level below that at which stories may be progressive because representational.

We must approach this problem by asking what sort of answer we need to the question of progressiveness in order to make significant progress. If I can deal with this preliminary question, I may not need to deal with the more awesome one.

In order to answer the preliminary question, I have to draw a contrast between narrative and nothing less than rationality. The essential point is that a contrast may be drawn, at least with a specific conception of rationality.

In a different context Richard Rorty discusses Heidegger's attempt to move beyond the terminus to "Platonism" marked by Nietzsche. "Platonism" is described as the tradition founded on the doctrine "that there is something independent of our inquiry and our language which we wish our language to represent accurately."[11]

Against this is the pragmatic view that "the function of language and inquiry is . . . to cope with the environment."[12] In the former view rationality is a kind of capacity or perhaps a procedure for getting things *right*. Thought and language, our representations of the world, must be rational in the sense of best portraying external reality. In this view rationality is our wherewithal for conforming to extralinguistic, extrainstitutional, ahistorical reality. In this way rationality contrasts with narrative, because the latter is inherently pragmatic and impositional in that as a presentation to the subject, the only standard a narrative must meet is productivity, whether with respect to mere survival or later to other objectives. At the conceptually elemental level it is organization that is critical, not portrayal. Association at this level is either a productive basis for action or it is not. Without begging the question against realism, such associations are not designed to conform to anything at all. Though again, this is not to say they are not causally determined. It is to say that while caused, they are not portraits of their causes or of some singular order in those causes.

Contrasting narrative and Platonic rationality brings out how the requirement that we explain narrative integrity is a thoroughly Platonic one. It is a demand for underlying associative principles. What would satisfy the demand would be an account of how individual narratives conform to a general pattern, how they conjoin elements in such a way as to be integrated and progressive in accurate portrayal of the integration and progressiveness of reality. But to accept this demand is to subjugate narration to Platonic rationality. And what I am maintaining is that we are *first* weavers of stories. We are not architects following divine plans that will let us structure our internal representations along the objective spars and girders of an autonomous and integrated subject world in virtue of the putative representational and referential nature of our thought and language.

Our authoring is not portrayal but imposition. We weave narratives and inhabit those narratives. What this comes to is that our narratives are prior to distinctions such as rational/ nonrational, true/false, justified/unjustified, grounded/ groundless, and integrated/unintegrated. Narrative is, as remarked above, inherently pragmatic. Its job in the first instance is to order experience. And the only standard it must meet is survival. To wonder about what integrates narratives, what makes them progressive, is to wonder how narratives "fit" something extranarrational, how they conform to something from which they borrow their character.

Nonetheless, it does seem that the integration and progressiveness of narratives are properties over and above sheer inclusion of some of the contents of awareness. There may be no Platonic matrix that lends narratives their integrity or progressiveness, but surely these are properties other than we could reasonably expect to arise from mere compilation. Even if we give up thinking of narratives as being what they are in virtue of being about something, we think there is more to be said.

Before saying all that can be said, I must look hard at the Platonic expectation. The central point of that expectation is that it is the conformity of narratives to an extranarrational reality that gives them integrity and progressiveness. This is a pre-Kantian assumption, and it tolerates only one alternative: that narratives not conforming to reality are precisely fictional. In other words, the implicit appeal is to autonomous sequentiality, to a reality having an intrinsic integrity. That integrity then is either captured or not, and if narratives are integrated and progressive in spite of not capturing external reality, they can only be fictional, literally fantastic, the products of fantasy. The integrity of fictional narratives will be borrowed from that of the imagination of their authors, from the integrity of the imaginative acts that produce them. The Platonic view, in keeping with the doctrine of transcendent essence, merely *circumvents* the matter of progressiveness by attributing it to an external reality.

The pre-Kantian conception, which persists after Kant, is that narratives can have integrity and progressiveness only derivatively. Against this the pragmatist wants to say that narratives have just the integrity or progressiveness that they have and that they have these inherently, not in virtue of something else. But in being a pragmatist, I need not deny realism in the sense of ontologically objective existents. What I deny is that those existents are integrated in the ways we take them to be or that some think reason demands. I am rejecting the objective orders of Plato and Leibniz. Once integration was internalized with Kant, ordered awareness was possible without metaphysical strings, and narratives could then be constitutive of order, though not, of course, thereby constitutive of existence.

What then of our feeling that integrity and progressiveness are properties of narratives over and above the sequentiality of their elements? I think that all that can be said here is that the properties in question are *retrospective*. It is how we see a narrative from a reflective, active perspective. More exactly, it is how *whatever* prompts responsive behaviour looks to us as self-aware, reflective subjects of experience. As to how and why some subsets of the contents of experience prompt action, while others do not—that is a question calling for philosophical and scientific theorizing well beyond the limits of my proposal.[13] Retrospective progressiveness and integrity are not cognitively temporally later than the initial presentation of a narrative. They will appear of a piece with what we are aware of, namely, experience as shaped by the narrative. But progressiveness and integrity are properties of our construals, not of the organizational sequences themselves. To understand this we must remember that a constitutive part of a presentation will be that its subject is inclined to act in some way or to refrain from acting. The alternative is the Platonic or Cartesian one, which disassociates action and judgment from a pure contemplation of representations or ideas. (I shall consider the role of imagination below, thereby clarifying the complex character of narrative presentation.) There are no properties of progressiveness and integration over and above what we make of experience. An organizational narrative is the beginning of action. Action is responsive but does not initially presuppose conceptualization as we now enjoy it, as is evident in the ability of even low life forms to respond to their environments. It is in this sense that progressiveness and integrity are retrospective. They are lent to what we encounter by what we do or are inclined to do about what we encounter, and later by reflection. At the nonreflective level there is only the bearing of action on what stimulates it. At the reflective level progressiveness and integrity are properties integral to our construals of experience. If we detached incipient action from a narrative presentation, we would be left with no more than a heap of objectifications and causally prompted responses.

In the relationship of *responsible for* we have a complex relational property that fairly clearly requires temporally later retrospective attention. It is a relation attributed reflectively, not simply responsively. That is, seeing one thing as responsible for another, or responsible for some change in another, is a matter not only of acting in some way but also of reflectively attributing special connection. Attribution or "perception" of the relation is a matter of focusing on what are taken to be the elements of progressiveness. The overall progressiveness of experience is taken to consist of chains of connections between individual items. Progressiveness is thought to be constituted by limited instances of relatedness. The importance of this is that the relation of *responsible for* is one that has traditionally been construed as the elemental determinant of the progressiveness and integrity of awareness. In a representationalist view it is the relation that supposedly best captures the putative integrity of reality; it is the crux of accurate portrayal, in that it is both what is most important to get right as well as what grounds awareness of the world and so is the basis of action. In my view *responsible for* is a retrospective and reflective relation, the "discernment" of which follows on action. We do not need the concepts of cause and effect to act, to deal initially with causes and effects. Animals and infants manage very nicely without these concepts, though there may be possible insistence that they have the concepts in some operational sense. But organizational narratives are available to us at a self-aware level only as integrated sequences in which the progressiveness presents itself as some included items being causally related to other included items. "Raw" organizational sequences are no more available to us as objects of awareness than are the "raw" data we conceptualize as the objects of awareness. We cannot, then, attend to anything other than as progressive and integrated in the sense of constituting events. But we must distinguish between behavioural responses to serially presented items and reflective construal of those items as causally interrelated. The former may be describable as acting on the basis of causal connection, but such action need not be preceded or accompanied by conception of causal connection. Infants grasp things long before they conceptualize them in causal terms.

I am suggesting a basically reactive conception of narrative integrity and progressiveness at least at the organizational level. Beyond mere objectification, experience consists of narratives integrated by our inchoate or actual action. Later we read into these narratives as essential properties what is only retrospectively theirs in the more basic cases. It is then that we can puzzle about how elemental associational sequences are integrated and progressive. And it is then that we puzzle about causal interrelatedness or the relation of *responsible for*. Admittedly I am dealing here with elusive ideas. In discussing what is conceptually elemental I must discuss what is unavailable to us. If I were making realist claims, the difficulty would be either insurmountable or require problematic "transcendental" arguments. But I am proposing only a way of thinking and speaking. Against the Platonic view, which casts how we are aware of the world in terms of internal portraits, the integrity of which is due the integrity of external reality, I am proposing that we speak of awareness as beginning with objectification, whether representative or creative. I want then to speak of the organization of what is objectified through sequences or collections that involve only some of those items and to cast these as the bases for action and as cohering in a special way because of actual or incipient behavioural responses. I then want to speak of retrospective, reflective assignation of responsibility in the causal sense. I want to call these sequences "narratives" because they are how the world is for someone in the sense that each is a presentation constituting an ongoing state of affairs. The fact that I am speaking of what is not accessible to us surely means that the more elegant account must be preferable. The Platonic or Cartesian requires all sorts of epistemological bridges and metaphysical pylons. Mine requires only minimal objectification and behaviour.

I am not proposing an idealist or phenomenalist scheme, for I am not impugning brute reality, only an alleged ordering of that reality that is reflected in our thought and language. I am proposing a "narrative reconstruction" of how objectification and behaviour are interrelated and result in our conceptualization of what there is or what we encounter as an ongoing, integrated sequence of causally related events making up a world.

But to continue my project I must now relate organizational narratives to full-blown narratives. Essentially I have to say how we, as storytellers, move from stories we act on to stories we attend to. The necessity here is to show elemental narrative employment continuous with more familiar uses of narrative.

Jean Piaget has described language as "much nearer to action and movement" for the child than for the adult, and described its employment in play in terms of something like self-defining commentary as well as a means "to bring about... what action... is powerless to do."[14] Initially the child is egocentric, even having difficulty distinguishing himself or herself from others. He or she engages in monologue which accompanies action. These monologues begin to have an effect on others, and those of others on the child, and there arises "adapted information". What happens is that the child begins to find parts of other monologues informative and is then prepared to engage in discourse. Piaget speaks of adapted information in a way nicely consistent with what I have said about organizational narratives:

> The criterion for adapted information... is that it is successful.... The function of language is no longer merely to excite the speaker to action. ...[As] Soon as the child informs his hearers... there is adapted information. So long as the child talks... without collaboration with his audience... there is only collective monologue.[15]

The genesis of discourse is collaboration. Prior to that collaboration language is merely an accompaniment to action. What interests me in this is that the shift from monologue to dialogue is not an *intentional* one. Reinforcement of a certain sort molds monologue into communicative dialogue. And Piaget's whole theory presupposes spontaneous monologue on the part of children, for it is that monologue that is the stuff of discourse, given collaboration by others.

I am presupposing not monologues but elemental narratives, but I want to tell a similar story, namely, that the move from utile narratives to full-fledged stories is a function of collaboration. What I need is a way of saying how narratives are verbalized so that they are responded to and the necessary collaboration occurs. The point is not to explain how narratives are externalized in the sense of being available to others. That much can be handled adequately enough with Piaget's account or something like it. My problem is more subtle. It is basically the matter of how we go from organizational sequences to fully linguistic narratives. It is the problem of going from presentations to descriptions. In a way this is the concern White has, which I mentioned above, of how we move from knowing to telling. My problem is complicated by philosophic tradition. In that tradition description may have two ontologically distinct subjects: presentations conceived of as perceptions of an objective world, and those same presentations conceived of as purely phenomenal. To the traditional philosopher, then, it will seem that the crux of my problem is how presentations, or the bases for action that I am calling organizational sequences, come to be so objectified that they can be the objects of linguistic description. Language development is construed as requiring accounts of how the world comes to be described, but in such a way that we also learn to describe our awareness of the world as something distinct. And much too often, philosophers have tried to account for description of the world as first description of the phenomenal.

The likeliest sort of account to be given here is one that will invite "private language" charges.[16] That is, it will be an account in terms of the association of sounds with features of our phenomenal fields. This is essentially the view of language developed by John Locke and more recently defended by D. M. Armstrong.[17] Philosophers worry about this account, because there are no public criteria for consistency of association, and because they cannot see how an individual's associations could come to be significant to another individual, that is, how the second would think of just those features which the first has in mind in making an utterance.

In some contexts the matter seems not to be considered problematic. The transition to description is taken for granted, and we encounter such claims as that "for children 4 to 5 years old, narrative language has become the prime medium of play. Thus, imagination is translated into literary imagination."[18] (What is meant here by "literary" is descriptive, narrational imagination and discourse.)

There is a lesson to be learned here. And it is that philosophers have too tidy a conception of the transition in question. The more productive construal of it is not that it is a sharp transition from responding to describing, but that, again as Piaget says, description grows slowly from linguistic accompaniment to action. One clue to this is that it is only in rather special contexts that description is "exact". More often it is embellished in a way that suggests the speaker is still very much bound up with the presentation being described. He or she is still in part defining what is being described, still shaping and fixing the experience. And here we have a hint of how telling stories for their own sake is not a phenomenon that follows description in being conceptually later, but rather precedes description in being world-making, largely as is elemental organizational narration.

Much of what I have been saying is supported by recent work on the part of Edward Casey, who has written on what I have been in effect appealing to much of the time: namely, imagination.[19] But the imagination Casey writes about is significantly different from what the tradition has taken it to be. Casey argues that philosophers and psychologists have consistently misdescribed imagining and imagination and either subjugated it to some other faculty or simply disparaged it as a bar to abstract thought, as a sort of conjuror of mental pictures. Plato saw imagination as a producer of mental copies; Aristotle and Kant gave it only a mediatory role in perception and cognition; Freud saw it as a kind of wakeful dreaming. Against this, Casey contends that imagination is central to conception and thought, that it affords much of the material for both, being in a special way an autonomous producer of "data":

> The autonomy of imagination is an autonomy of freely projecting and of freely contemplating a proliferation of pure possibilities. . . . it is by autonomous imagining that consciousness comes to know itself in its multifariousness. . . . Imagination multiplies mentation.[20]

Imagination as described by Casey both helps to clarify my proposal about organizational narratives and supplies much of what I need in considering the externalization of narratives. Imagination is not only the provider of imagistic content and a link between sensibility and understanding. It functions to smooth and complete experience, to enable us to envisage events, to employ alternative bases for action; and it involves a certain spur to the extension of its own use. The comprehensive role of imagination that Casey argues for is in fact that of supplementing and complementing sentience, of organizing and integrating experience. And the enrichment of thought processes also includes a reciprocal enriching of the role and use of imagination.

Casey remarks that imagination involves an element of "self-enchantment".[21] Without imagination we would be uninspired problem solvers, assuming we survived. We might even lack self-awareness. But with the ability to multiply mentation we become more than competent. The autonomy of imagination invites its use beyond what is necessary for behavioural efficacy. Gardner tells us that imagining is indulged in by children "for the sheer enjoyment of representational activity."[22] Though I must here say "presentational", in line with my proposal, we see new force in the passage quoted earlier from Gardner about narrative language becoming the "prime medium" of play. And here we find what will prove crucial to a discussion of selectivity, below, which is intended to resolve reservations about the transition to description. We see that the creative aspect of narrational activity is pleasing *in itself*.

We enjoy the making of realities for ourselves and others. The externalization of narrative is prompted and reinforced by pleasure. And it is here that we must shift our focus of attention from narratives generally to fictional narratives in particular, for it is these that become most important to understand in proceeding. The reason is that the key to the continuity between organizational sequences and more familiar narratives is the production of nonutile presentations in a deliberate way—in other words, storytelling.

Constructed presentations, being what they are, are enjoyed as possible worlds or possible states of affairs. That is, there is no need to wonder how stories come to be of interest and how they come to be valued. That would be necessary only if they were wholly novel in kind. They are just more of the same, more world-making done now for its own sake and reinforced by the collaboration of others. The difference is that we know better than to act on the basis of these new presentations or narratives. But that does not preclude our enjoyment or our identification with the agents with whom we populate these narratives. In fact, it enhances our enjoyment, though much of a responsive nature is left intact. Anyone who has cringed in vicarious embarrassment on reading a book or watching a movie will appreciate this point, as well as its supportive implications for what I have been proposing. As to the production and appreciation of nonutile narratives, what I want to say is that the production of fictional narratives is like learning to dance. It is like turning locomotive bodily movements into something that is embellished in a special sense.

But embellishment presupposes selectivity. The selectivity at work in producing fiction is a focusing on what pleases. In dance, for instance, fluidity of motion, which is more or less incidental to locomotion, is focused on and developed to a degree that would actually interfere with mere locomotion. But that focusing and development result in the delineation of an activity. That is, parts or aspects of a broader activity are grouped as the elements of a special activity. And this need occur only a few times, for once others encounter it as a special activity, they are free to participate in it without creating or delineating it anew.

What is there about narration that can be embellished as fluidity in motion can be? Before I can attempt an answer, I must say how narration comes to be recognized as an activity some aspect of which can then be embellished.

Surely one of the first things we must notice is that some narratives work and others do not. We constantly adjust our stories in light of new experiences. We seem quickly to come to feel that things will go well with us only if we get our narratives *right*, only if they match something external to them. We are, in other words, launched on the search for truth, for correspondence between our narratives and a putative reality. But the process of having narratives "go wrong" focuses our attention on narration as something we do, as opposed to its remaining something that occurs but does not become an object of reflective awareness. We may not conceptualize the activity as producing narratives; we may precisely think of it as producing and employing descriptions. That we come to think of the productivity of narrative employment as due to correspondence to "reality" is incidental. What matters is that we acquire a category for narratives that are not fit bases for action when some fail us. We begin to compare narratives, to wonder if one or another is reliable, to hope that one is. And we begin to recognize lies. And in the process of developing this category, we begin to recognize narrative employment as an activity.

The recognition is accelerated by personal or historical disillusionment with the power of narrative to fix events. Prior to conception of a causal order governed by immutable laws, there would be no compelling reason to preclude attempting to influence events through narrative. The only perceived problem would be how to go about it, how to give narratives priority over events.

Given the idea that narration may fix events, it is a short step to narration for the sake of creation. We can understand the taking of that step in terms of attempting to fix reality and coming to like the results of our efforts. For the primitive to whom agency is the only explanation, narration must appear simply as a mode of agency. The exercise of that mode would be unthinking until experience finally overwhelms the expectation of efficacy. Consider cave paintings. Against the common view that they celebrated past hunts, they seem to have been intended to set the course of future hunts. They were not depictions but optimistic "predictions" almost certainly thought to have at least a chance of determining how things would go. But the paintings themselves came to be appreciated independently of their putative efficacy.

Even after experience has taught us that our stories have little or no power to determine the future, once we categorize narration as an activity, we become enamoured of the production of narratives for their own sake. We are enchanted with our ability to create a kind of reality. And we learn to appreciate the doing so by gifted others. What begins as part and parcel of coping with experience, and is naturally extended in play, is first noticed, then exercised as an effort to determine events, and finally comes to be practiced for its own sake. Worldmaking for its own sake is selected out of what we do in coping with experience. And then we begin to appreciate such world-making by others, so much so that most of us largely stop doing it ourselves. We come to be entertained by world-making, and our entertainment is reinforced by novelty and the absence of effort on our part. The manner in which we select out world-making for its own sake from the way we define a world out of experience sheds important light on the difference between "factual" and "fictional" narratives. And in better understanding the fact/fiction distinction, we begin to see more clearly how organizational narratives are continuous with more familiar narratives.

By casting ourselves as natural narrators, as initially organizing experience through organizational sequences or narratives, we establish a continuity between such narratives and more familiar stories. This precludes difficulties about understanding "fiction", but it has import as great with respect to how we come to differentiate "factual" and "fictional" narratives.

Children seem initially to distinguish stories from "factual" narratives in terms of distance ("Once upon a time...", "In a kingdom by the sea...", "In a galaxy far, far away..."). Distance in time and space suffices for appropriate response. And it is in terms of responses that we must understand the difference at issue, not in terms of a "correspondence" relation. The received view is that it is the nature of narratives that determines our responses. I am suggesting that it is the nature of our responses that determines what is "fact" and what "fiction". The difference between the two lies not in the contrast between referential and nonreferential language or narrative but in types of responses to narratives, in the differences among answers to the question "What should I do?"

The most productive understanding of the factual/fictional distinction is a pragmatic one. There is no initiation into a special language game of pretended reference. We begin with narratives some of which prompt action and some of which do not. Talk of "real" and "made up" begins on two fronts: First, some narratives prompting action are productive and some not; second, some narratives, such as those intended to influence events, come to be valued for their own sake. Unproductive narratives and those valued for their own sake are classified as somehow separate from real (read "pressing") events. Even these, though, may influence action or condition perception. This point clarifies the ambiguity of how myths are taken. It is not that myths are half believed or cherished as fantastic but effective behavioural guides. Rather they are narratives calling for diffused responses. They call for action conditioned in certain ways given certain circumstances. Myths approach being abstract narratives. But it is on the basis of our responses, by acting or not, that we differentiate among narratives. And we are helped along first by liars and later by philosophers and theologians.

Given the distinction between the pressing and the non-pressing, we begin, now decidedly with the help of philosophers and theologians, to make the distinction between sorts of narratives as one between realms. The factual/fictional distinction begins in how we take narratives, in the ways they pose situations for us, and in our responses. But it soon is made into a distinction among the subject matters of narratives. In short, a pragmatic difference is made into an ontological one.

To return, then, to the matter of continuity between organizational and more familiar narratives, we must appreciate the "emergent" nature of the fact/fiction distinction and the manner in which we progress from employment of basic narratives to the construction and enjoyment of more complex ones. We then see that there are no hard distinctions to be drawn among kinds of narratives. Moreover, the view that descriptive or reporting narratives are paradigmatic and basic must be seen as misconceived. It is a view that presupposes both that some narratives can mirror an extranarrational reality and that as such these narratives constitute the basic form from which other narrative forms derive. Against this, the matter of continuity should be seen as a nonissue, for questions about the continuity of organizational and more complex narratives can arise only if we accept one of the more complex forms as both basic and different in kind. The real support for the view that narrative is primarily a reportive mode of presentation, as opposed to simply how we cope with experience, is the distinction between fact and fiction. Given this distinction, whatever is thought to capture "fact" assumes a special importance and priority.

The rejoinder to my remarks will be that whatever one does in response to a narrative about centaurs will simply fail or constitute so much random behaviour, behaviour that will not relate to anything. Against this, responses to narratives about an ongoing or impending tidal wave will prove productive. But this rejoinder begins with a sharp distinction between "real" things and "imaginary" ones and then classifies narratives as either about one or the other. This insures that responses to narratives of the latter sort will be fruitless, or at least fruitless in certain circumscribed ways. And the fruitlessness of the responses is then assigned to the lack of referents for the narratives. This looks acceptable until we look more closely. First, my thesis is about language and the organization of experience. The rejoinder is about what there is and how language allegedly "hooks up" to what there is, how it accurately portrays what there is, while some uses or parts of language fail to hook up to anything at all. Second, the rejoinder presupposes an adequate understanding of the relations of "correspondence" and "reference".

I do not intend to deny reality, to make the world belief- or language-dependent. I am denying that there is a general, understood, and reliable way to differentiate stories about the "real" world from stories somehow about nothing at all. Matters are more complicated; there is very little that is fixed and determinate to which we can relate descriptions in a tidy, one-to-one way. Most of what interests us is at least in part a function of perspective or is attitudinal and escapes unproblematic portraiture.

But what should be evident is that the rejoinder presupposes institutionalized stories and story characters, like tales about centaurs and personages like Sherlock Holmes and the Minotaur. It trades on a rich cultural hoard of narratives to which responses are conventionally determined and on characters conceived and introduced as "unencounterable". All of this supports the common illusion that we can always tell the "real" from the "made up", that all our responses to narratives are either to factual descriptions or to "fictions", that the only question is whether a problematic narrative does or does not describe "reality".

It must be appreciated that it is not brute reality that is at issue here but its alleged reflection in language and our access to it. My proposal turns on acknowledgement of the interpretive latitude for world-making allowed by the way we deal with experience. If our narratives, elemental or otherwise, are circumscribed and determined by "states of affairs" and are "correct" or otherwise, if they only mirror "how things are" at their best and are simply wrong at their worst, then human life and experience are much simpler than they appear, and interpretive parsimony must always be a failing. It must be like a broken camera the shutter of which allows less and less to be imprinted on the film. Against this I want to describe interpretive parsimony as a decline of creative or innovative construal of something not sufficiently fixed to allow portraiture. This is why I have taken a pragmatic stance, to disallow that awareness is accurate or inaccurate in ways that language allows us to differentiate in virtue of "correspondence" and "reference" or their failure. I want to stress how we use language to shape experience, not how experience must conform to language as a medium for portraying reality. Only then shall we be able to understand the complexities of human experience and our ways of coping with it.

To conclude this chapter, I must say more about my pragmatic position. The need to do so arises because what I have been saying about narratives suggests strongly that narratives will be successful bases for action precisely when true or factual, and I want to say that the fact/fiction distinction is one that is drawn after the initial employment of narratives in the ordering of experience.

The main obstacle faced in trying to understand the fact/fiction distinction pragmatically, and hence narratives as prior to the drawing of the distinction, is what gives the distinction its grip: namely, that it seems inescapable that some narratives are about real events and others not. To deal with this obstacle I must consider two points. One has to do with how we can in fact connect bits of language with bits of the world; the other has to do with appreciating how slippery the fact/fiction distinction actually is. I shall consider the second point first. Scrupulously "factual" descriptions are often unhelpful and "fictional" or partly "fictional" ones very helpful for understanding people and events. Furthermore, we seem unable to maintain the distinction in many areas. Perhaps the clearest cases are those where the narratives or accounts describe human relations. In the case of two people reviewing a marriage, one may describe it as happy while the other inventories the trials and problems. Each is emphasizing aspects, half discerning, half imposing patterns, and in effect deciding to see the marriage in one way or the other. There is no possibility of comparing the narrative and the "actual" events. There just are no objective events, as each will be what it is because of attributed significance. Courtroom situations abound in examples of this sort. Even the reading of a supposedly factual police report into a court record shows that being "factual" is a matter not of faithful replication but rather of careful neutrality with respect to the interests of the parties involved. Actually, "factual" usually has more the sense of "fair" than the largely philosophical sense of representationally accurate.

In large areas of our lives we seem never to attain a purely referential use of language, for we seem unable to identify anything as a pure referent. And when we come close to doing so, as we shall see, we end up only with ostensively definable items and with little scope to say anything interesting. The response will be that nonetheless, at least when we are engaged in describing physical things present to us, we are sure of our referents, and that sureness is all we need to ground our distinction between talk about real things, such as Conan Doyle, and fictional things, such as Sherlock Holmes.

But when we look closely, we find that all of this cashes out in terms of our being able to relate certain sentences, which are bits of the world, to other bits of the world and that what matters is our responses, what we do with or about sentences. To say this is not to deny hard reality; it is only to express bafflement at what "reality" comes to beyond what we do.

The issue here is not reality but the distinction between language that is allegedly "about" it and language that is allegedly not. But we have no access to the relatedness, so no basis to make the distinction in terms of "aboutness". Brute access to brute objects will not do. Fingering a coffee cup in a philosophy seminar is one thing, and encountering the Minotaur in a story is quite another. But the point here is that *whatever* the difference, it is not one mirrored in language in virtue of "reference" or its lack. The difference between two narratives is not that one "hooks up" to things like the coffee cup and another fails to or, worse, hooks up to a ghostly Minotaur. The difference is what we do with them. What we must resist is a view of language as consisting of two idioms, one connected to the world and the other not.

My pragmatic thesis is less a denial than a comment on the fact that the "correspondence" relation between (true) sentences and real things and events has never been made out. We can better explicate the distinction we draw between the factual and the fictional in terms of what we do with and about narratives.

With respect to how we relate sentences to things or events, whatever else it may be, pragmatism is not a theory nor an analysis of truth. If it were a theory or analysis, it would be open to the charge that seems to haunt my proposal, namely, that effectiveness or "warranted assertibility" (Dewey) or utility is precisely due to truth.

Pragmatism must be seen as an alternative vocabulary, a shunning of "correspondence" and "grounding". But pragmatism of course allows us to relate bits of language to bits of the world, such as sentences like "The cat is on the mat" to the sinuous Siamese on the boukhara. What is eschewed is the idea that the sentence is "true" in virtue of the cat's relation to the rug. The relation between the sentence and the cat on the mat is a juxtaposition, not a "grounding". And it is *we* who establish it. We have the illusion that in staring at the cat on the mat and uttering the sentence we are at least very close to an ostensive case of "correspondence". But we never break out of language. We never succeed in putting ourselves at right angles to the "correspondence" relation. It remains something we bestow rather than something autonomous.

We do class together sentences that we do not pair with bits of the world. But we should see that this has to do with intentions and responses not with an absence of "referents" for sentences in a special language game. The mistake is to think that pairings of sentences and bits of the world are achieved in virtue of preexisting relational possibilities, that there are "facts" waiting around to be portrayed in language, and that language has a unique capacity to portray facts, as film emulsions have the capacity to retain images. "Fictional" sentences are simply noninstrumental, and the classic error is to think them noninstrumental because fictional.

The feeling may persist that factual and fictional sentences do, after all, differ in some intrinsic way because of their referents. My account of the difference in terms of responses may still look as if it collapses into responses differing because factual and fictional sentences differ in the way the traditional view says they do.

But this question cannot be *answered*, because it is not a question; it is a perspective that presupposes Platonism and so precludes pragmatism. Rorty remarks that

once we take the step from Plato to Kant, from correspondence to coherence theories of truth and knowledge, we are no longer responsible to anything save ourselves. Once the "realist" conception of objects waiting around to be accurately represented goes, then nothing is left save utility.[23]

But we *have* moved from correspondence to coherence; language now is "an instrument for getting what you [want], for imposing your will on the environment."[24] The above question presupposes that it is still possible to think of language replicating something and hence that the best way of understanding differences in responses to sentences is to think in terms of differences among the sentences. This view requires that we know when we have sentences of one or the other sort independently of responses to them; hence all the philosophical efforts to find a criterion for truth. The view at issue looks viable in the abstract, and our prejudices are with it. But it simply has never been made out. Neither the correspondence relation nor a criterion for truth has ever been adequately formulated. To echo Rorty's general message in *Consequences of Pragmatism* and *Philosophy and the Mirror of Nature*, "representationalism" just has not worked, and it is time to change the subject, to abandon an unproductive philosophical discussion.

So far I have sketched a proposal for speaking about the organization of experience in terms of narrative employment. I have tried to establish a pragmatic continuity between an elemental activity and a highly developed one. The heart of my proposal is that elemental organization of experience be construed as narrational, as integration of items from sentience and imagination into progressive sequences through action and reflection. Cognitivists think we are "hardwired" to organize input spatiotemporally and causally. To suggest that narratives are elemental is to suggest that the way spatiotemporality and causality are applied to the sensuous manifold is by including phenomenologically prominent items in sequences that constitute presentations of situations and as such simply are the world for each of us.

My proposal does face general philosophical difficulties, such as making out the pragmatic position against correspondists and referentialists, but even these are problematic as difficulties. They are difficulties only against the backdrop of the current conception of philosophy and the current philosophical commitment to "representationalism," or the view that knowledge and language reflect a determinate reality. It is against this backdrop that narrative is construed as a special mode of cognitive presentation, a special cognitive game. That this philosophical view coincides with popular conceptions is not to be counted support for the philosophical views but rather is an indication of the influence since Plato of academic philosophizing on popular views.

My proposal stands or falls with efforts such as Rorty's to undermine received philosophical opinion and to make out the pragmatic position. The reason is that otherwise the continuity between organizational narratives and more familiar narratives would have to be made out, in terms not of a productive vocabulary but of an actual continuity between *pre*sentational activity at an elemental conceptual level and reportive, *rep*-

resentational activity at a higher level. However, I cannot hope to settle the debate between pragmatists and correspondists. I can only present arguments that may make my proposal plausible.

3

Interpretive Parsimony

In this chapter I must say how my narrative employment proposal relates to interpretive parsimony as well as how interpretive parsimony in turn relates to aging. I shall attempt
to accomplish both objectives by making clearer the notion of
interpretive parsimony.

The previous chapter was devoted to explaining how we organize experience narrationally, to showing that narrative is
not a devised mode of presentation but a natural extension of
basic conceptualization. Narrative is not even the sort of universal code that people like Roland Barthes and Hayden White
take it to be. It is of a piece with the most basic way we have
of structuring awareness. I am not interested in merely using
the notion of narrative heuristically to understand the organization of experience. I want to treat the notion as elemental
and hence its application in the discussion of, say, literature
as actually an extended use.

My objective in chapter two was to articulate a pragmatic
proposal that construes the use of narrative as a basic activity
that is continuous from the most elemental structuring of
awareness to the production of stories. I now want to construe
our adaptive capacities as in part functions of that activity of
narrative use. Essentially I want to say that the taking of
something as a situation is an imposition of narrative structure.

Taking something as a situation and behaving in some way

are two sides of the same coin. At times this will be evident in that construing something as a situation *is* to respond or to begin to respond in a given way. This will not be so in all cases, but it will be so at the unreflective level, wherein to be conscious of a world is to be disposed to act in specific ways. The lack of reflection may be due to the primitive nature of the case, but it may also be due to occasional absence of self-awareness in spite of its occurrence at other times.

If I can make my proposal plausible, I shall then be able to construe perspective narrowing or the inhibition of adaptive capacity in terms of overly parsimonious use of narrative. And the advantage will be that such construal of interpretive parsimony will enable us to see at least some of it as a function of organizational success over time, rather than deterioration due to time.

The connection between interpretive parsimony and aging is that whether for good or bad reasons, aging and interpretive parsimony seem closely tied in expectation and to some extent in fact. It is my objective to make out how this latter connection is best understood as due not to deteriorative factors but to success in the parsimonious management of experience.

The reason that age-related expectations of interpretive parsimony are worrying is that they result in the elderly, who are the minority, ceasing to be participants in the conversations that constitute culture and becoming objects of discussion. Of course there is a reciprocal "reduction" of the young from participants to objects on the part of the elderly, but because the elderly are the minority, it is they who bear the burden of the negative consequences of mutual reduction.

What I want to do is understand at least some increase of interpretive parsimony, or decrease in adaptive capacity, in terms of success in adaptation, as opposed to as a consequence of inevitable deterioration. The result I seek is that perception of the elderly by the young, as well as their self-perception, change for the better. The main way this betterment may come about is if the young and the old stop seeing themselves as separated by a gulf of an extraneous nature and see whatever separation there may be as a result of how we organize experience. The other side of this is that the old will not perceive themselves as distanced from the young by something beyond their control and hence something that they must bear. The old can come to understand that at least part of the distance is due to something that is attitudinal and hence open to revision. In short, they can see themselves as excluded from conversation for reasons that have to do with what they bring to conversation, not by what they are or come to be simply by growing older. We should then begin to deal with the special difficulties that biological age brings in a more neutral manner, as we now do the physical handicaps that affect but do not thereby lessen human beings.

But to proceed I must acknowledge a rather special problem generated by my enterprise: namely, the matter of how to prevent my own consideration of interpretive parsimony from deteriorating into objectification of a group of human beings who happen to be chronologically older than the present majority. The fact is that my interest in perspective narrowing must focus in a special way on the elderly, for they are the ones who suffer most from assumptions about and the actuality of such narrowing. But the point of my enterprise is to detach perspective narrowing from aging *as such* by explaining how it is related to aging.

Earlier I noted that it will not do simply to exercise greater care, to have greater concern with respect to the elderly. We ought not to think in terms of a class, "the elderly", not in the sense that we consider its members to constitute something like a natural kind. References to age should always be of a particular sort and relate to some specific need or condition. It is relevant to mention someone's age as seventy if our interest is in heavy physical effort. It is not relevant to mention age if it is done to mark attitudes and assumptions of a prejudicial sort, even if these appear harmless or are even couched in complimentary terms: "She has a sharp sense of humour and she's nearly eighty!"

Not thinking of older people as "the elderly" is tied to the reason why my proposal is not an answer to a delineable "problem" and so amenable to empirical research. The proposal is conceptual and aimed at improving our culture in a general way by facilitating inclusion of all reasonably competent human beings as equals in the activities that constitute culture. Our present ways of speaking and thinking mark off parts of the population in invidious ways. In particular those among us who are in their sixties or older are seen as a specially problematic class characterized by traits assumed to be due to deteriorative processes that are a function of the sheer accumulation of years.[1] Articulating a "problem" in this area would inevitably mean retaining what is central to these ways of speaking and thinking, namely, retaining the objectification of the more senior among us as "the elderly". What we need is not adjustment or correction of our ways of speaking and thinking but complete revision. And I am also convinced that the greatest bar to such revision is the assumption of a necessary connection between perspective narrowing and aging as such.

Along with racism and sexism we can count "ageism", a prejudicial attitude toward those over sixty or so that distances them from many aspects of our form of life. This attitude is abundantly evident in otiose references to age that presuppose that advanced age is always a significant factor in description of one of our fellows. Expression of ageist prejudice masquerades as clarification. References to age (or gender or race) are usually offered as amplifications of an innocent sort, but the motivation is often prejudicial. In the case of ageism such references reinforce the objectification of a group of people in terms of presumed perspective narrowness and debility. The result is that individuals of sixty or more become objects of prejudice simply on being recognized as of advanced chronological age.

However, it would seem that I am myself objectifying the elderly. I have in effect excluded the old from my conversation by discussing them as an object group. For one thing, I suppose that as a forty-six-year old, I have been unconsciously addressing other forty-six-year olds. Someone twenty-two or seventy-two reading this book may well have felt that long before this juncture. And the seventy-two-year old will certainly feel that she or he has been cast as an object of discussion and not as a participant in conversation.

What I propose is that references to "the elderly" and similar expressions in what follows be read and understood as references to chronological age strictly. It is, after all, my intention to break the connection between references to chronological age and implications of interpretive parsimony. But the point is not to do away with the former. We cannot hope to improve anything by avoiding references to chronological age. The point is to detach pejorative connotations from those references. When need arises to refer to those whose adaptive capacities have declined, I shall speak of the "interpretively parsimonious". But this is a clumsy phrase, so for brevity I shall use the shorter "parsimonious". It will be clear from the context that I am speaking of those with reduced adaptive or interpretive capacity and not of misers.

But now let us turn to the matter of what it is to be parsimonious. The parsimonious get that way by succeeding at what parsimony is all about, the ordering of experience. This sort of success may be exemplified by considering how a teacher may learn to anticipate the questions most students might ask in a particular course. Such anticipation is a way of ordering and making manageable what the teacher encounters in a typical working day. For a time he or she will be successful in anticipating questions and will seem rather formidable to the students. But students change more rapidly than teachers like to acknowledge. Soon the questions will be somewhat different. The teacher who continues to anticipate the same questions then begins to appear inflexible and perhaps even arrogant. He or she will be relying overmuch on the success met with earlier and may even come to think of certain questions as the correct ones to be asked. Effectiveness will begin to suffer. But instead of responding to the changes, the teacher is likeliest to blame the students, usually in terms of exaggerated contemporary concerns or poorer preparation. In effect he or she will fail to see a decrease of success as due to his or her practices. Parsimony then impedes effectiveness rather than facilitating it, in that it conditions perception and reinforces the practices in question. But what must be noted is that the teacher became parsimonious because he or she did in fact successfully anticipate the right questions for a considerable and formative time. It is the success met with that prompts confidence in identification of a range of likely interests on the part of students and that precludes extending or changing that range. The teacher organizes his or her encounters with students in terms of certain anticipatory classifications and responses. However initiated, these persist because of their initial success. And when that success diminishes, the fault is attributed to other factors because of the entrenchment due that initial success.

A comparable situation is a writer who begins to be restricted by a number of plots and characters because of success met with in using those plots and characters. The writer may even recognize the need for change but be unable to shake free of what he or she has used before. We think of this as a failure of creativity, but it is better thought of as the constraint of productive habit on creativity.

It is usually difficult to meet challenges with novel responses. We rely on what has worked before, and when it fails to work, we blame other factors. As noted earlier, it is probably more productive over the long run to trust previously successful methods than to be forever trying new ones. And we are inclined to be more suspicious of situations than we are of our methods for dealing with situations; this inclination is also due to success. The teacher and the writer in the above examples are trained, as an animal is trained, by success, by "reinforcement" that fixes responses to situations.

But my concern is not only with responses, on which one tends to focus. More important to me is the perception of something as a certain sort of situation. Logically, and sometimes temporally, prior to responses are the construals of situations, the categorizations of what we respond to. When certain responses are rewarded or reinforced, the construals that prompted them are rewarded and reinforced. The heart of interpretive parsimony is that ways of construing what we encounter are continually selected by the success of our consequent responses. And hence adequacy of response may result in too much reliance on too few and too familiar ways of construing situations or ordering experience. Every time a familiar response proves satisfactory, there is selection against new construals and therefore against new responses.

Consider a more complex example: Suppose our concern is with the ineffectiveness of traditional language training in imparting fluency. It may well be that stress on grammar and syntax results in perception of the employment of language as the conscious application of a formal system. While their native language competency will not be affected, students may come to see the speaking of any other language as not spontaneous in the way that speaking their own language is spontaneous. And the construal of a foreign language as a formal system is reinforced because good grades are contingent on getting grammar and syntax right. But the student will not learn to speak the new language fluently, for using a language is not a matter of the conscious employment of a formal system. Yet it is just that construal of the new language which is selected by academic success. One of the broader consequences is that the special idiom of a science may be perceived in the same way, and we may find that a student's difficulties with French or German result in difficulties with physics or physiology. The student may unconsciously see the mastery of a technical vocabulary as he or she does the learning of a new language and so may be impeded from making progress in various courses. The student moves from being daunted by a foreign language construed as a formal system to being daunted by anything involving an unfamiliar vocabulary.

In my example the parsimonious factor is a matter of generalizing from how a foreign language is presented to how anything involving a special vocabulary should be construed. Even operating instructions for complex equipment may be seen as unmanageable formal systems that require mastery in themselves prior to successful application. Such a perception will preclude experimentation and "hands on" familiarization and hence will preclude competence, to say nothing of facility.

The requisite success factor is present in the language case in that what is rewarded in the traditional method is precisely mastery of the grammar and syntax of the object language as a formal system. In this example it is clear how one may be explicitly taught to perceive something in a certain way and reinforced in doing so. And the result is not only lack of fluency but inhibition in the learning of anything that resembles a language in some crucial respect. Here we have imposed categorization of the sort that, for better or for worse, is inevitable in educational contexts.

The examples of the teacher and the writer show us another aspect of parsimony, namely, self-directed categorization and consequent success. But in both sorts of cases what happens is that something encountered is taken in a particular way and certain responses are deemed appropriate. And in both cases success met with reinforces the perception of whatever is encountered, whether that perception is imposed or self-directed.

However, in all three cases it is somewhat wrong to say that responses are taken as appropriate, for we must appreciate that to structure what is encountered in one way or another is to begin to respond in specific ways. This is a large claim that requires fuller treatment, and much of chapter 4 will be devoted to it. At this juncture it is enough to make the bare contention, to be filled out below, that in at least some cases there is no conceptual or intentional gap between construal of a situation and responses to it.

But it is a fair question to ask what all this has to do with narrative employment.

Recall that the advantage of talking about interpretive activity in terms of narrative employment is that we can then understand the construal of situations in particular ways in terms of the use of narrative or, more precisely, the imposition of narrative structure. As organizational narratives are elemental in world-making by virtue of presenting us with situations carved out of experiential chaos, at more advanced levels narratives also serve to constitute more complex presentations or realities by a similar, though more complex, imposition of structure. Of course there will be nothing deliberate in this imposition, as it will be a matter of seeing certain events as taking place, certain individuals as interrelating in given ways, and so on. Structuring experience, then, is being described as imposing narratives. And growing parsimonious in the ways we structure experience is being described as growing parsimonious both in how we employ narratives and with respect to the narratives we impose.

But so far I have offered only a kind of metaphor, and I need rather more than that to pursue understanding of interpretive parsimony in terms of ever more restricted and restrictive imposition or employment of narrative.

To proceed I must stress how central to our lives and activity it is that our awareness of the world is of "ongoingness". That is, our perception of our environment, and of ourselves in that environment, is inherently active. This is what was so notoriously missed by classical empiricism, which tried to capture "ongoingness" in terms of sequential presentations of data. But such presentations notoriously failed to yield a world. The phenomenologists and some psychologists tried to remedy matters by stressing the gestalt nature of the objects of awareness, appealing to such phenomena as the way we perceive motion in seeing lights going on and off in sequence. These efforts may have been adequate to counter empiricist theories of perception, but they do not begin really to capture the fact that awareness is active through and through.

And how is the activeness of awareness best characterized? If we find such examples as flashing lights a little flat, how might we put things better? I think that here I can simply reiterate what I have been saying: We have our being in stories, in ongoing narratives. The apparent simplicity or unanalysable nature of the notion of narrative is due precisely to its conceptually elemental role. We are hard put to say what narrative is, because to do so would be to say what awareness is.

A typical sort of psychological test involves being shown photographic slides and being asked to tell what is going on. The objective may be to test for consistency of interpretation and identification with persons portrayed. Each slide is presented as a frozen moment in a series of events involving two or three people. The test proceeds on the sound assumption that nothing out of the ordinary is expected in asking that a still picture be "expanded" into an ongoing situation. We tend to see still pictures as bits of ongoing events, at least until we learn differently. Children often ask what is happening when they see an interesting picture. In our culture still pictures usually depict some moment in an ongoing series of events. And it is the mark of artistic or photographic talent that the moment depicted approximates universality with respect to some type of ongoing situation. It is perfectly natural to provide the earlier and later "stages" that turn the picture in question into something like a frame in a movie that depicts a developing state of affairs.

We are, as was suggested earlier, like computers programmed to weave what we encounter into ongoing stories. We work what we find in awareness into developing situations. We perceive things as components of ongoing activities. We perceive others as agents, and to be an agent is to be engaged in ongoing projects. We perceive events as consequences of agency or as bearing on agency.

The notion of a narrative as an account of a series of events, as a particular presentational mode, actually captures our active natures when conceived of as a developmental organizational device, in contrast to more familiar static devices such as categories. And here we have something of a rather peculiar nature. We are able to understand activity of an elemental sort by considering an activity of a very much higher order. The parallel is to the way we may understand citizenship by considering naturalization.[2] In the special case we see explicitly the requirements and obligations that are only implicit in the standard case. In like manner, we may better understand elemental organization of experience by using a notion that has its more natural, or at least more familiar, place in quite sophisticated activity, namely, deliberate storytelling.

What is given in experience is woven together by fitting people and events and things into what we can think of as preexisting story structures. However, these structures will not always preexist; sometimes they will be developed in the process of dealing with something. In both cases what occurs is that the items encountered in experience are dynamically juxtaposed and interrelated. These juxtapositions and interrelations survive as patterns in the sense that dispositions persist to juxtapose and interrelate new items in the same ways that have proved productive. I am calling these patterns "narratives" not just to compare them, as dispositional patterns, to familiar stories but also to capture their essential developmental and organizational nature.

I want to use "narrative" to discuss the structures or patterns that abstractly describe dispositional activity as well as the way in which those structures or patterns present themselves to someone whose world they define: as ongoing situations. These patterns, when described in the third person, are like printed computer programs that describe what a computer does or will do. I am somewhat less interested in the actual running of the program, in the sense of what someone may be actually doing, for the questions that raises are basically practical ones. My main interest in considering narrative imposition and parsimony centers on the narratives that capture what is presented to the agent as a situation, though not necessarily at the reflective level. The behaviour that results is of secondary importance. However, "narrative" captures both, in that the term denotes the program that the activity follows, as a response, as well as how items in experience are related and identified, or what the behaviour is a response *to*.

Each time an individual encounters an unfamiliar situation, and copes by imposing a familiar narrative structure, that individual is reinforced in the employment of that structure. The result of this is that the more success is met with in active categorization, the more likely the individual will be to employ that same categorization again. The trouble is that at some point the tendency to rely on familiar narrative structures will begin to inhibit novelty of response and construal. This need not occur, of course, but it will occur more often than not. Our inclination decidedly is to rely on what has worked before, and it is a fine line between productive reliance and unproductive overreliance.

One thing that should be obvious is that time is an essential requirement for the parsimonious process in question. That is, there must be sufficient experience to allow for enough success to result in overreliance on familiar categorizations or narratives. And it will be even more obvious that satisfaction of this main requirement means that most of the individuals who come to be overly reliant on a limited set of narratives will be those among us who are older. An important consequence of this is that one of the categories in narratives used by younger people will be of older people as more restricted in interpretive or adaptive capacity. This will follow from the simple fact that younger people will have dealings with older people in whom interpretive parsimony has become evident. The main link between parsimony and aging is that it takes time for success in coping to make us overreliant on stock construals and responses. My teacher and writer examples show that time is essential for the development of parsimony; and as time passes, people age. Unfortunately, in common thinking age is a cause of parsimony, whereas age is only a necessary condition of parsimony.

Thus far I have relied on the intuitive clarity of three examples to suggest the nature of parsimony and its development. I have relied on intuitive clarity with respect both to the structuring of experience by the imposition of narratives and to parsimony as restrictive and restricted narrative employment. And I have relied on intuitive clarity in saying that what underlies the connection between parsimony and aging is that the former takes appreciable time to develop and become evident. But intuitive clarity will take me just so far. I must further clarify parsimony, and to do so must say a good deal more about what it is that we come to use parsimoniously.

A number of points must be amplified at this juncture. First, I have spoken of narrative employment in referring to dispositions to juxtapose and relate items in experience. These dispositions constitute presentations of situations to us; they are determinations of the world in being particular responses to how the world is taken to be. Second, I have spoken of narratives to describe what is reflectively available to us of these dispositions, that is, the ongoing situations presented or the world as objectified by our imposition of order. Once these impositions occur, once they are "enacted", we retain the patterns of these impositions, or the structures of these narratives. The patterns are then available to us to deal with consequent experience and hence are what may come to be used parsimoniously. My first point is fairly radical, for it precludes that there is nonbehavioural construal of situations at least at some levels. (No "seeing" that is not "doing", to twist the Wittgensteinian dictum that there is no seeing that is not seeing-as.) But it is the second point that poses the immediate difficulty, in that to make out parsimony more clearly I must say how it is that these patterns or narrative structures may be thought to be retained and so to preexist whatever they organize. They will, as noted, not always preexist what they organize. But some must, or else my proposal would have little point, as it turns on parsimonious use of preexisting structures.

Our form of awareness is best construed as essentially narrational; conceptualization is best thought inherently narrational in the sense that experience is organized into ongoing sequences. This means that at some level we must postulate available structures into which we fit what we encounter. The alternative would be that new structures are imposed in every instance and that similarities between structures are coincidental. This alternative seems very unrealistic and somewhat repellent. Creativity on this order looks too much like madness.

How, then, might narratives be said to be retained and be available for employment?

Coping with the contents of experience in terms of juxtapositional and organizational dispositions can be called "responsive construal", and it is just this that I am calling narrative employment or the organization of experience by the imposition of developmental structures. When such a structure is employed, its pattern is retained. And reliance on some of these patterns may become excessive; we may become overly parsimonious in using them.

In infancy an individual deals only with a few other individuals who gradually come to be identified as agents separate from self, paradigmatically a mother and a father. The identification in question involves first imagistic and emotional factors and later linguistic factors. Slowly the individual begins to extend his or her characterizations to include others beyond the mother and father. Small children often embarrass their mothers by addressing strange men as "daddy", and the child's response to negative feedback consequent on the error is paradigmatic of the process of extending his or her insufficient set of categories.

Clearly aspects of initial identifying activity will condition extension of such activity. How the mother is perceived emotionally may, to a greater or lesser extent, condition the individual's perception of all women, so much so that relations with women may be hampered and therapy of one sort or another be required. This sort of preexisting categorization is familiar to all of us and has been inescapable since Freud. However, there is a tendency to understand it in terms of static categories. At least some aspects of it must be understood in terms of developmental devices or narratives. For instance, from the point of view of the very young child other males must be distinguished from the father, rather than the father being noted as one male among others. But this does not occur in terms of the addition of new, static categories. That would be too sophisticated a process. Instead it occurs in terms of new and extended narratives, albeit of a very simple sort.

What occurs in the child's immediate environment establishes the norm. Its own, the mother's, and the father's activities are categorically primary. These goings-on prompt and constitute the child's first narratives. There is then need to distinguish and deal with the activities of others, beginning with siblings and other members of the child's immediate group. Eventually still others must be dealt with. Doctors are first "fathers" who do annoying things. After they become "non-fathers", they are for a time identified more or less exclusively in terms of those annoying things and certain salient characteristics. Hence a barber or a florist in a white coat will be expected to poke one or to stick a needle in one's arm. The child is proceeding on good empiricist principles. What is less obvious is that it is doing so not in terms of static categories but in terms of narratives in which persons in white coats just do annoying things. We must get away from the overly sophisticated idea that a child perceives a man or woman in a white coat in the rather abstract manner of someone disposed to act in certain ways. The child perceives the person in question in terms of specific imagined activity. Seeing the figure in a white coat is not a matter of attributing dispositions; it is a matter of envisaging the doing of particular things. When children are asked what they are afraid of with respect to apparently threatening persons, they invariably answer in specific terms: "He's going to stick me!" or "She's going to poke me!"

What we have here is like an ongoing story that is activated by something encountered: a person in a white coat. The story is a developmental category. It is available as a set of dispositions to juxtapose and relate items in experience, a set pro-

ductively thought of as a pattern into which something can be
fitted and so made sense of, like a person in a white coat.
I am trying to bring out that static categories are insufficient.
At best they would support static ordering. What is required
beyond simple pigeonholes is active "categories" that enable
us to organize what we encounter in terms of ongoing characterizations. And this is why narratives are basic to our form
of awareness. They enable us to organize experience actively,
developmentally, ongoingly.

But active devices for organizing experience are retained,
just as static categories are retained once employed. We *learn*.
Once a narrative has been imposed, it may be reimposed. Once
a narrative has been used, it becomes a constitutive part of our
experience, just as a category or concept is thought to be acquired. The process of dealing with experience is thereby the
process of coming to be equipped to deal with further experience. If we acquired only static devices, we would make no
progress.

I am contending against the common notion of static categories as exhaustive. But whereas I want to broaden our scope
in this respect, I want to narrow it in another. I want also to
contend against the equally common view that behavioural
dispositions are general and to reconceive them as considerably
more specific. The common view of dispositions is a vague one
of inclinations to behave in ways broadly characterizable by
certain descriptive terms, such as "irritably", "pridefully", "op-
timistically", and so on. Somewhat more specific are notions
about how people are apt to behave in certain types of situations. For instance, someone might be expected to panic under
pressure or to become defensive when pressed on some matter.
But I am arguing for much greater specificity that renders
dispositions more comparable to particular skills. A trained
surgeon or technician will deal with what is presented to them
in given contexts in quite specific ways. What they do will be
done in a certain order, it will bear on particular things, and
so on. And often they are not able to say readily how they
proceed. What they are doing is following set operational patterns that have been honed and refined over a considerable
period of time, but without necessarily being reflected on or

articulated. What we think of as dispositions are seen to be considerably more specific than usually thought when we pay close attention to the contexts in which they are enacted and when we follow the behaviour in question in those contexts. Dispositions then look more like skill-patterns.

I am trying to understand active, developmental organization of experience in terms of imposition of structure and behavioural dispositions of a fairly specific, context-determined sort and then am trying to understand both in terms of narratives. I am thinking in terms of particular organizational impositions that constitute presentations of ongoing situations and in terms of the behavioural patterns that constitute responses to those impositions. But impositions and dispositions, or presentations and responses, are the same in some cases. This is because at a basic enough level construal of something as an ongoing situation just is acting or beginning to act in particular ways.

It might now be claimed that I can say everything I have said without speaking of narrative employment, or that if I do speak of narrative employment, I do so only in a metaphorical or imagistic way to accentuate what I am saying about construals, responses, and organizational dispositions.

But to make this claim is to miss the thrust of what I have been saying. The point of speaking of narrative employment is to conceive of organizational impositions as available narrative structures. By using the notions of narrative and narrative employment, I am deploying a pragmatic vocabulary that enables us to deal better with conceptualization in terms of the imposition and employment not of static categories but of developmental structures. These structures are being introduced as narratives that order the elements of experience, that organize these elements as goings-on and the components of goings-on. The nonintentional employment of such a structure is the imposition of a retained narrative on experience, and a "playing out" of that narrative, and thereby a coping with what is encountered. Sometimes new narratives will be created in dealing with experience, but such creation will be clearer once I have said how narratives are retained.

My general objective is to understand parsimony in terms of

restricted use of narratives, so as to better understand how parsimony can be a result of something other than just growing older. The immediate problem is to make out how narratives persist and are available for use. This is actually less a matter of propounding theory than of clarifying how we might think of their persistence. My aim is to hammer out a viable vocabulary. The project is comparable to Freud's description of dynamic psychological elements and processes, which had practical, therapeutic value but was never intended as description of actual neurophysiological elements and processes—though some further identification with such items was envisioned. The clarification sought, then, is a matter of getting clear on what moves to make, not of better illuminating "actual" processes.

I shall proceed by resorting to some rather artificial means of characterizing narrative employment. A narrative structure, in analogy with a computer program, will be thought of as an ongoing, developmental structure or algorithm that allows varied interpretation of variables. Call these narratives or structures "plots". The variables may be characterized in a very limited way as place-holders for what will usually be agents and fairly circumspect actions. Call these "characters" and "doings", respectively. I am here using ordinary terms in order to reduce the air of artificiality as much as possible and to highlight the naturalness of the proposal. It must be remembered, though, that I have a certain latitude within which I can distinguish my uses of these terms from their mundane uses.

I shall speak of "standing" plots and of "new" plots; the latter designation conveys that a plot is new in that it is worked out in the process of dealing with something perceived as a novel situation. All new plots become standing ones, though this does not entail that they are always employed or retained if not employed. The distinction is primarily between a plot available for employment and one worked out in the process of coping with a situation.

Plots are standing plots in that they are available for organizing phenomena encountered. An example is the way some people cannot encounter a married friend with an attractive person who is not the friend's spouse without construing the relationship as morally suspect. We might think of this as a culturally determined and simplistic plot of a prejudicial sort. What is unclear is how such a standing plot is retained so that it may be employed again and again.

We can imagine an abstract structure that results in anything that meets certain criteria being juxtaposed to something else in a set way. We would usually speak here of dispositions or, as a psychologist friend does, of "well worn interpretive grooves". But grooves in what? And, unless we are Ryleans, what persisting states support the dispositions? My psychologist friend thinks that the grooves in question are often-used neurological connections, but to so think presupposes making out a correlationist or identity theory. And I cannot make my pragmatic proposal contingent on the success of a metaphysical program.

Parsimony is a matter of overreliance on too few standing plots, characters, and doings. But this means that plots and their variables may be greater or lesser in number. And if I cannot have recourse to neurophysiological "traces", I must produce a plausible conceptual model of how plots persist.

I might here have recourse to rules and suggest that a standing plot is like a set of instructions of the following form: "When a situation encountered involves elements of type A, B, and C, take elements of type A as related to elements of type B in X way, and take elements of type B as related to those of type C in Y way" ("When encountering a married male friend with a woman who is both attractive and not his wife, take their relationship to be . . . "). But the example brings out two things: the general character of such instructions and the fact that it vitiates my general proposal about narratives and conceptualization, for narrative employment here is clearly rule-governed. To be rule-governed, narrative employment must be intentional. I might argue that it may be rule-governed at some levels, and not at the more elemental level I considered in chapter 2, but this will not do for two reasons: First, the rule idea actually makes the notion of narrative employment redundant. That is, it would be of only heuristic value to call the construals produced by such rules "narratives". Second, the intentional character of rules or instructions would preclude continuity between unreflective narrative employment at the elemental level and reflective narrative employment at other levels.

How else might I characterize narrative employment? Let me return to the computer analogy. A computer program is a set of instructions but not a set that is followed intentionally. To describe a program as instructions just means that we can map it out on a machine table that shows how a given state will lead to another. A program is the quintessential step-by-step sequence. The computer's singular advantage is that it can take the multitudinous steps very very quickly. It can afford to deal with everything in terms of highly specific instructions. (And anyone who has used one knows just how specific instructions are and must be.) The language of the computer is binary, and instructions are really nothing more than the toggling of switches and series of switches.

Unfortunately the computer analogy serves only so long as we think of computer programs as the sorts of "programs" that we ourselves use. And it is just these that I am trying to understand. However, the computer analogy does provide me with one device, the nonintentional implementation of instructions. What I can borrow here is the idea that we can speak of instructions being implemented, or of a program being applied, nonintentionally, without it being held "in mind". When we begin to learn how to do something, we keep in mind fairly large chunks of instructions and implement them when we identify something to which they apply. But computers do not envisage programs or parts of programs while running them. They proceed from state to state, "oblivious" of everything including their progression. It is only given a particular state that another state is entered into, in virtue of the configuration of the prior state.

Our trouble may well be that we are too wedded to the idea of intentional application and so fail to see that the employment or imposition of narratives is much more like the strictly causal workings of the computer. Therefore, it is not necessary to think of standing plots as retained in mind if we acknowledge that plots are not necessarily intentional structures. And this is as it should be, for some narrative employment precedes reflective awareness and occurs at the level of conceptualization, so plots are not available to us as something to employ. Only their results are available to us, as the reality we face.

However, this is not to say that we cannot come to understand that we do organize experience narrationally and hence might learn to exercise some measure of indirect control over that organization. For instance, when we are alerted to the fact that we tend to act prejudicially toward some individual or group, we can consciously review how we take that person or group. In fact, we might describe interpretive parsimony briefly by saying that it is precisely failing to realize that the process of narrative organization occurs, and so not understanding that we gerrymander experience into convenient shapes, and hence forgoing control over the process.

But it seems, then, that it is not necessary to provide an account of how standing plots are retained, at least not as intentional structures in the sense of being had in mind as we may have a scheme or scenario in mind. A standing plot is really an abstraction, like a machine table, that describes a series of moves. Unlike a machine table it will not be very tidy, and it will have some open dimensions, but the parallels are more significant than the disparities. But while I may not have to explain how plots are retained as plots, what about the "nature" of standing plots? How are we to think of that? Many will demand to know what they *are*.

The tendency to expect that something can be said about plots in terms of their nature must be resisted. Even if I could successfully argue that they are neurophysiological traces, little would be gained. What we must understand is how they function. To say that a standing plot is this or that "in the order of being" will say little or nothing about how it works. My interest is not in theorizing about the order of being; it is in reconfiguring the "order of knowledge", in reshaping perspectives and ideas.

Behind the concern with what plots might be in themselves is the expectation that they must be like rules in their operation. But while we must allow that plots have abstractable structures, plots do not preexist employment of plots as sets of rules. I have spoken of narrative employment as dispositions to juxtapose and act on items, but this is to be understood as employment of structures that preexist only as specific patterns, not as general rules for the guidance of behaviour. Newly encountered items are fitted into particular juxtapositional and relational structures. These are structures that obtain as consequences of prior productive employment, as opposed to being learned or abstracted rules.

It used to be an educational-psychology slogan that "the response that occurs is the response that is learned" (Guthrie). The point was that what an organism initially does in a given situation is what it learns to do, and training must focus on reinforcing approximations to correct behaviour. The corollary is that undesirable responses must be treated as learned and as requiring active obliteration, because nothing is simply forgotten. The relevance of this slogan to my proposal is that plots are acquired in just this way; we learn to do what we in fact do, assuming perceived success. What is retained is the particular narrative structure that either proved productive or was so perceived. The agent does not learn rules by which to construct plots; he or she learns the particular plots.

Plot use, then, must not be thought of as an intentional activity centering on the application of rules to experience. For one thing, at some levels of conceptualization, what such rules would be applied to are themselves the products of narrative employment. But if plot retention is not to be dealt with in terms of an account of the nature of plots, as intentional structures or neurophysiological traces, what can be said about how plots are stored?

All I can do here is appeal to our understanding of habits and skills. Knowing how to ride a bicycle is something that persists, but not as a set of rules or as an envisaged activity. We say that we just know how. A good diagnostician knows how to do his or her job without necessarily having any idea of how he or she proceeds or how learned patterns persist, whether as neurophysiological traces or, to echo a passing remark once made by Arthur Danto, as ghostly inscriptions on the flanks of a *res cogitans*.

The fact is that I do not face a special difficulty with regard to plot retention. I need only assimilate plots to habits. This may be to group the obscure with the murky, but my proposal about narrative employment is no worse off than our ordinary talk of habits. Actually, my plots are very close to what are described as "habits of mind". References to these are readily understood and such habits are often a subject of interest, as when we try to instill good study habits or to change unproductive ones, and they are thought no less real or important for the elusiveness of their nature.

It is tempting here to have recourse to linguistic ability, and notions such as that of "deep grammar", to amplify how we manage to have habits of mind. After all, many of these are linguistic. But if our understanding of ordinary habits is incomplete, notions like deep grammar are even more problematic for being theoretical. Another temptation is to replace rules with metaphysical devices, to follow Heidegger, for instance, and use the notion of *vorhabe* or practice as a fundamental one and then to preserve its mystery by declaring it inaccessible. This is not an appealing option for a pragmatist, but the Heideggerian notion of a practice that is not reducible to or renderable in propositions is a useful one. All I must do to avail myself of it is eschew the metaphysical implications. A practice in this sense is something that is retained, but not in the sense of possessing rules. And practices of the sort in question are precisely specific. They allow a certain latitude in application, but they are coherent and determinate wholes, and not as sets of instructions or rules are. The latter's unity is of a different order in that it consists of relations among propositions, whereas the unity of practices consists of relations among actual and potential actions.

It might be noted at this juncture that the retention of rules is as mysterious as the retention of practices or plots. There is no advantage to rules in this respect. And rules, as was said above, have the disadvantage of requiring that a good deal be clarified about how they are applied. This is because their application is intentional and yet is not always evident. Narrative structures need not be applied intentionally; they are not retained as are envisaged schemes or rules available to reflection (though this is not to preclude that some occasionally might be).

Plot creation is not rule-governed either, nor is it intentional except in advanced cases. To be rule-governed, plot creation would presuppose both intentionality and second-order rules for the application of first-order ones. And this would in turn presuppose prior conceptualization of what newly created plots organize, which would be self-defeating as well as raise all the old questions about basic conceptualization. Plot creation is simply occurrence and imposition. And selection among new plots is not in terms of conformity to rules but in terms of productivity. It is intrinsically consequential.

The latter point raises the matter of "realism". Part of the significance of plot use and plot creation not being rule-governed is that plots do not conform or fail to conform to anything. We do not have Platonic or other transcendental directions for replicating reality, for bringing ourselves into line with "how things are", for "getting it right". What we have are ways of coping. Whatever reality is, it is precisely dealt with and apprehended by the imposition of plots. The "shape" of elemental plots is determined by neurophysiological, psychological, and anatomical factors. Later, cultural and historical factors also become determinants of plots. But while plots are certainly causally influenced, they must not be thought of in some Platonic way as mirroring their causes or conforming to reality or failing to do so. If it seems remarkable that human beings are as consistent as they are in their organization of reality, that is because we are human beings and are very alike in ways that we understand. There is no need to attempt explanation of such similarity in terms of something further, such as rule-governed internal replication of reality.

But as indicated in chapter 2, I am not denying realism. What I am denying is that we are equipped with the means to replicate accurately an inherently structured reality by producing internal representations of that reality. All we can say about reality is that we are able to cope with it by "representing" it as we do, that is, by imposing the plots we impose.

In the coming to be of a plot or a practice, as in later employment of one, a person construes the world a certain way in responding to it as he or she does. The response may be tentative and variously adjusted, or it may be practiced (though not necessarily proficient or effective). But in either case it is integral to awareness in that it is at least in part constitutive of what the person is reflectively conscious of as his or her world or some part thereof. As such, the plot in use is not an applied set of rules or the like, but a specific way of being and acting in the world. It is something enacted, a "running" program.

The preceding clarifies what I want to say about the difference between a new and a standing plot. That difference is basically that a new plot is one that has not been previously enacted. Whether its component parts are themselves new or have individually occurred in other plots is incidental. The gestalt that is the plot in use is novel as a gestalt. And the corollary is that a standing plot is not novel in that it has been previously enacted as a gestalt. How a standing plot is stored is a question for theory. It is sufficient here that the requirements of my proposed conceptual scheme are satisfied by saying that a standing plot is one previously enacted in an agent's career and hence is a constitutive part of that agent's operational history.

One further point is that in the case of an adult, plot creation cannot always be productively told from adaptation of standing plots. It is so told only in the fairly rare and clear cases where previous experience with something is simply lacking. While we may often feel it more productive to consider something to be plot creation as opposed to adaptation, as when prior experience is missing or when consequences are extraordinary, it seems to be a very fine line indeed between dealing with something new in new terms and dealing with something new in refashioned terms. It would appear that evidence of plot creation, as opposed to adaptation, has to be consequential; it must follow behaviour that indicates novelty of a sort requiring ascription of new plots as opposed to only adapted ones.

The difference between plot creation and adaptation is important with regard to a basic misconception about parsimony and aging. It is too simple to think of parsimony in terms of the failure or inhibition of plot creation. Too much of what we do in dealing with the world is plot adaptation, or cannot be told from plot adaptation, to accept the widespread assumption that originality and interpretive flexibility are always "creative". The older among us are thought to lose the ability to be "creative". But the opposite of parsimony is not prolifigacy of sheer invention, as seems to be assumed. Parsimony is in a sense more a loss of judgement, of the ability to tell when adjustment of response is called for.

The relation between parsimony and aging should now be clear: The development of parsimony requires considerable time and experience. But I want to reiterate that parsimony is a product of success, or at least apparent success. As reliance on standing plots increases, fewer new plots occur, for what is encountered is dealt with more and more in familiar terms. There are no new responses and hence no new plots. But increased reliance on standing plots should not be conflated with a dearth of new plots or seen as a consequence of a dearth of new plots. It is not that failure of creativity leads to fewer new plots and hence greater reliance on standing ones. Rather, greater reliance on standing plots inhibits the production of new ones. Older people are seen as somehow unable to generate new plots for various physical and psychological reasons. But in fact what occurs is that a lifetime of success or perceived success leads to overreliance on the familiar, to parsimony, and that inhibits plot creation. In other words, the factors that result in the inhibition of plot creation are not extraneous to plot use. Inhibition results precisely from success met with or imagined. The popular notion that creativity somehow dissipates or is used up with age attributes a false property to us and then deprives us of it as we grow older. What we lose is not a mysterious power but *practice*. We stop fashioning new tools because the old ones serve us well enough.

Parsimony is, quite simply, a product of operant conditioning. And it is incompatible with extensive plot creation, for the latter occurs only when needed. Parsimony is not a matter of lost potency; it is a matter of lost practice due to adequate competence in dealing with experience. But because construal is of a piece with response, in dealing with experience in familiar ways, we actually bend experience to our expectations. Perception comes to follow practice, as we might put it. In this way diversity of actual situations does not suffice to insure plot creation through need, for that diversity need not be perceived as such. If we can speak at all of objective diversity of experience, it will always yield to interpretive habits. Because plots are imposed, diversity of experience is a product, not a stimulus. Of course plots may prove unproductive, may in some sense fail to deal with reality, but they are never wholly determined by reality, except perhaps for a few very elemental ones occurring at an early age.

The picture I have been painting is of parsimony as essentially a growing conservatism of an interpretive and behavioural sort. The main difference between this picture and the common view is that in my view the increasing conservatism is not the effect of aging but rather is an accompaniment to aging. It is a result of simply coping.

I have introduced the idea that conceptualization is of a piece with behaviour, at least at some levels, and that it therefore consists, in basic cases, of the enactment of behavioural patterns more specific than usually thought. The specificity is due to the nature of the narratives that constitute both how we respond to the world and what we are aware of as the world. I have spoken of narrative "employment", but it has emerged that there is nothing intentional in this, so far as my present concerns go. In the next chapter I shall pursue these points with a view to developing my pragmatic proposal. My aim will be to make my proposal: that parsimony is restricted and restrictive narrative employment, not only a kind of picture of perspective narrowing but a scheme useful for understanding and dealing with perhaps the most distressing aspect of aging.

4

Plots and Conceptualization

My proposal about narrative employment and parsimony is a pragmatic one in that I am not claiming to have *discovered* anything. But the proposal does require adjustment in our way of thinking; in fact the proposal is intended to change our way of thinking, particularly about aging. The proposal's point is to provide a new conceptual matrix for construal of perspective change over time.

In this chapter I shall focus on how plot use constitutes conceptualization and hence how restricted and restrictive plot use results in perspective narrowing. The first thing to clarify is how conceptualization should be construed as more specific than normally thought.

In speaking of the specificity of plots, I should not be taken to be somehow precluding individual concepts or categories. The plots in question are describable as patterns of application of individual concepts or categories. That is, the sense in which narrative employment is being identified with conceptualization does not preclude the abstraction of individual concepts or categories. What it does preclude is that applications of individual concepts constitute the determinants of how the world is for someone and are prior to behaviour.

The distinction I am drawing is not unlike that drawn by Wilhelm Dilthey in rejecting Aristotelian and Kantian categories as determinants of conceptualization. Josef Bleicher, in describing this aspect of Dilthey's thought, puts the point as follows, in part quoting Dilthey: Concepts or categories are not "mere tools of thought . . . but 'the structural forms of Life itself, which, in its temporal process, finds expression in them'."[1] Narratives are not collections of individual concepts. They are the "structural forms" in which our dealings with experience have their being and are manifest. But these structural forms may be "parsed" into individual concepts and their application. What I want to reject is the idea that the application of individual concepts or categories could, in itself, constitute awareness. It is part of the Cartesian madness to think that we are capable of being aware of a world which, whether ideational or objective, presents itself as an intelligible composite. The thrust of my talk about narrative employment is that we fashion our worlds. That fashioning may involve the use of "tools of thought", of concepts or categories, but that use is an active, integrated imposition of narrative structures, a shaping of reality within the bounds of causality. It is not a recognition of a *this* and a classification of a *that* and then a deliberate series of Cartesian acts of will that determine what we do about the *this* and the *that*. Consider a simple example. "Friend" and "foe" are individual concepts, and they admit of deliberate, reflective application, as when someone is reviewing the actions of an acquaintance. But treating someone encountered as either a friend or a foe is a matter of acting in a certain way. It is a way of acting that constitutes a pattern that determines choices and behaviour. We tend to think of treating someone as a friend as a matter of acting in accordance with a certain classification. But the classification surely follows on the behaviour. The individual concept, "friend", is culled from behavioural patterns. This is clear in ordinary life when we find ourselves *acknowledging* that someone is a friend.

The picture, then, is one of basic behavioural patterns that in being enacted constitute construals of what the agent encounters. Only later do we abstract individual concepts. To play on Wittgenstein's advice about not asking for the meaning of something but asking for its use, I suggest that we should ask not about concepts but rather about what is done. *That* is what tells us what and how the world is for someone. Of course as we become reflective and our behaviour becomes very much more complex, things begin to look different. We begin working with more and more individual concepts because of the complexity of what is presupposed by our behaviour. At more advanced levels, every single act will be set in a rich context of assumptions and distinctions. This means that it will become much more difficult to identify individual plots in use. For one thing, there will be a good deal of overlap. For another, reflective influences will be at work. But this difficulty does not mean that plots are not in use. It is simply another instance of the contemporary acknowledgement in the physical and social sciences that we cannot always isolate operational elements without distortion.

The immediate objection will be that my proposal would require an impossible store of specific plots, as well as equally impossible selection devices for the employment of those plots; and the latter would be required despite the fact that such "employment" was not intentional.

But it seems no more implausible to suggest that we store specific patterns than that we store complex rules. And the selection devices for specific patterns surely are no more mysterious than metarules for the application of rules. Specific patterns and causal selection devices are also more easily accommodated neurophysiologically than are rules and metarules. The former can be physical traces, whereas the latter cannot if conceived as intentional in nature. Moreover, plots are not all of a kind. They vary greatly in scope and hence in specificity of application. The objection construes them as of a kind and tidily circumscribed.

The pattern imposition I am calling narrative employment is conceptualization in that it initially determines how the world is for someone as that individual responds to stimuli in patterned ways. But when behaviour grows more complex and incorporates more plots, and when reflection introduces new dimensions, these plots or patterns become multilayered. Some will have subplots as components. And plots overlap. The consequence is that, as noted, plots become difficult to identify *as* plots. That is why we think in terms of individual concepts and categories. We lose sight of the forest and focus on more readily

identifiable trees. And because we habitually think in terms
of individual concepts, we consider it absurd to suggest that
our thought and behaviour can be adequately dealt with at any
level in terms of specific plots or narratives. But that is precisely because we have lost sight of larger trends. (Therapists
become very good at rediscerning these. They point out to their
clients that the latter, say, deal with people defensively or too
aggressively or that they pursue goals too obsessively.) Concepts are to plots what letters are to words and sentences. We
cannot speak or write in letters, only in words or sentences.
Nor can we think or act in concepts. Thought and action, and
their diversity and novelty, cannot be understood in terms of
individual concept-elements.

Individual concepts are "tools of thought", but they are not,
as it were, thought itself. Conceptualization may be construed
as the application of individual concepts, but that is a very
sophisticated and abstract notion. It does not do justice to the
richness of concept use, to the ongoing, developmental activity
from which individual concepts are abstracted. Surely this is
what is wrong with the mechanical character of Aristotelian
and Kantian category employment that Dilthey sought to ban-
ish. Such category employment always sounds as if it is engaged in by an individual who already possesses at least minimal
conceptualization. And that is precisely right. The sort of specificity of behavioural patterns I am arguing for is in fact a
necessary condition of concept use. The application of concepts
cannot be a "bootstrap" phenomenon, as seems generally assumed. There must first be behaviour. And behaviour must be
specific in just the ways I am suggesting. Human beings do not
initially open concept-guided observers' eyes on a neutrally
objectified world. They see a world in terms of their goals and
desires. At first they are agents immersed in an environment.
They distance themselves from that environment only when
they begin to reflect on their interaction with it. To describe
their initial interaction with the environment as involving concepts is to speak in the abstract about the particular bearing
that action has on the environment. It is a way of describing
operant construals. But such description does not entail that
the way those construals are operant is as the application of

concepts possessed prior to action or in any significant way separable from action. Here we must think of human beings just as we do of animals, to which we would not be tempted to ascribe concepts as such or their intentional application. Perhaps I can make things clearer by describing plots as operational structures. Unlike the commonly conceived application of a concept, an operational structure is determinate in a special way. Concept application, as usually construed, seems to require intentional recognition of the satisfaction of certain criteria. The latter is the point that has always plagued the notion of a concept as a recognitional capacity, namely, the need for recognition that certain criteria are satisfied prior to the application of a concept. This raises the problem for empiricists that if concepts are acquired by observing similarity, it seems that they must be possessed to make possible the recognition of similarity. The alternative has usually been thought to be the rationalist one of making concepts innate, which is a most unappealing option as we understand neither how it might work nor even quite what it means. But the fact remains that intentionality haunts the traditional concept of a concept. The how of application remains mysterious. We should, of course, be thinking in terms of *imposition*, but the trouble is that many see that as jeopardizing realism, a condition that they find unacceptable.

When we forgo intentionality and abandon the notion of concept application, except as an abstract description, things look more manageable. An operational structure can be thought of as determining nonintentional or reflex behaviour. And in doing so it is, though itself caused, impositional as opposed to recognitional. An operational structure is impositional in the sense that both the causes that elicit its operation and that operation are nonintentional. Once given its operation, what is intentional or available to reflection is the result of the structure's operation. The agent is conscious of a world shaped by that operational structure.

An operational structure will work on whatever comes along, as we might put it. Against this, concept application is like a set of instructions and seems to require discernment or construal of something as a fit object of application. Plots are precisely operational structures in that they are impositions of order, as opposed to being discernments of order. They do not, at least initially, involve deliberate application.

If it is argued that concepts may also be applied unintentionally, then I think we are in fact dealing with operational structures. In such cases "concept" is appropriately used only in referring to an abstraction from some instance of behaviour, just as in describing a computer program we say that the computer is "following" the rule: Always hyphenate between identical consonants. But the computer is not following anything at all; it is proceeding according to an operational structure. Whenever it is typing a line and it encounters a margin and identical consonants, it will hyphenate. The computer cannot follow a rule, because it cannot entertain a rule or recognize when a rule is applicable. What it "recognizes" is a certain concatenation of signals. These are an encountered margin and identical consonants to us, but to the computer they are so many specifically configured binary bits. Computers paradigmatically are operational in an impositional rather than a recognitional sense. This is evident when they make a hash of something because wrongly prompted. And we must not confuse responsiveness to causal cues with recognition.

Operational structures nicely capture the nature of plots or narratives. They catch precisely that nonintentional dispositional character that makes narratives or plots basic organizational devices, as contrasted with devices requiring intentional application to what then must already be conceptualized and organized in some way. Whatever a plot operates on is not identified and organized prior to that operation. The emergence of something as a situation encountered is precisely a product of plot imposition. At least this is the case at the elemental level at which plots or narratives serve as organizational sequences. Later, when there is room for reflection, there is intentional discernment or something closer to concept application.

The components of behavioural patterns are initially reflexive. These are "bits" of behaviour, particular responses, which become elements in more complex behaviour or in what we recognize as action. Human infants are innately equipped with very little. They reflexively grasp what touches their palms, they reflexively suckle when their mouths are touched in a given way, they reflexively blink, and so on. But there are a number of psychological reflexes, too. We can imagine one being feeling pleased when smiled at, and another feeling badly when yelled at. And each of these will involve responsive behaviour, albeit of a simple sort, for instance, smiling, frowning, crying, moving toward or away from something. The psychological adds a dimension of depth to overt behaviour and allows for an exponential growth in complexity. Even changes in the sequence of behavioural elements would make for diverse responses, but of course human beings are capable of much more complicated element configuration. Given such possible complication, it is not hard to visualize the beginning of quite sophisticated behavioural responses even with relatively few elements. And the "internal" view of these responses, from the point of view of the agent/subject, will be even more complex because of memory, expectation, and the superimposition on behaviour of psychological elements in varying degrees of dominance.

The preceding is a sketch of how narrative organization of experience begins in reflexive responses and is quickly complicated and formalized in ways that result in complex adaptive behaviour. Later, self-reflection further enriches the responsive mix, and we can begin to recognize what we presently think of as characteristically human behaviour. Later still, we characterize our thought and action with the help of abstractions, especially that of the application of concepts.

In my view, then, early plot creation is really a matter of the amalgamating or coalescing of individual bits of reflexive behaviour into fairly complicated responsive action. And of course each resulting behavioural complex will itself be available to serve as an element, in whole or in part, in new and richer behavioural complexes. In this way it is not long before there is impressive diversity of behaviour, which is further enriched by reflection. But before there is conceptualization in the sense of the application of individual concepts, there is patterned behaviour; before there is categorical conceptualization, there is plot use.

However, it must be remembered that this is a pragmatic proposal. I am hoping that psychological and other theory will support my proposal, but I am primarily concerned to sketch a way of thinking about how we operate. As such, my proposal need only be compatible with contemporary theory. I am not concerned either to offer a competing theory or to support present theory in any technical way.

What should emerge from the above is that the matter of how plot use constitutes conceptualization is primarily one of how concepualization is first *doing* and is only later categorization as a special sort of doing. Basic conceptualization or initial plot creation is just coping with experience. Plots come to be simply in the agent interacting with his or her environment. And by just surviving, the agent generates the wherewithal for continued survival, for new plots become standing plots. Whatever actions the agent performs in coping establish repeatable patterns of behaviour. And because the actions performed will be performed in certain contexts and involve extensive associations, they will not be general enough to require maintenance as rules for acting. They will be maintained as specific patterns. The trick comes in their further application in contexts that are somewhat different from those in which they arose, and it is just here that we begin to see the differences between more and less productive plot use and also between agents who are more and less restricted in plot employment.

Admittedly it does seem counterintuitive that we are possessed of numerous plots for acting. But we should recall how, when learning something, we work at having it become "second nature", at coming to do whatever is in question more or less automatically. In learning a skill, we strive precisely to adopt a pattern of behaviour. It is in just this sense that we speak of acquiring a skill. We mean that we come to possess it, to have it as a pattern of behaviour that requires little or no conscious effort in its exercise. In fact we count someone more competent the less he or she has to think about what he or she is doing in a particular context. We should also recall how often we find ourselves dealing with someone or something in a set way, so much so that we must strive not to do so: not to treat ex-students as still young undergraduates, not to treat childhood friends too familiarly. And how often do we catch ourselves saying of something newly encountered "Oh, that's just . . . " and likening it too readily to something familiar? Sometimes we are right, of course, and sometimes we are not, but we do constantly run up against our dispositions in this way. And those dispositions are almost invariably matters of employing standing behavioural patterns, fairly specific patterns of behaviour. That we refer to these as "habits" and "skills" suggests that they are exceptional in being specific patterns, that most of our behaviour is not set in this way. But this is an illusion, one evident in the manner in which we assess others. Invariably we do so in terms of quite specific patterns of behaviour.

We simply should not expect to gain much insight into how we operate by attending closely to how we think or feel we operate. It is inevitable that part of operating in one or another way will be thinking and feeling that we operate in a given manner. And the reflective construal may or may not provide the most productive description of that operation. For one thing, it will certainly include self-protective elements. And more generally, it will be couched in the theoretical terms of our time and place. We may ascribe "humours" to ourselves, think ourselves possessed, see our actions as historically inevitable or determined by phrenological factors. In each case plot use is itself construed in particular plot terms. Our self-understanding is always the product of our time, and so our perception of our own workings will be as structured and gerrymandered as first-order objects of thought and action.

As I sketched above, narrative employment is construal and response; it is conceptualization that is inherently behavioural. It is not application of concepts and consequent action but rather is patterned behaviour from which individual concepts and categories are abstractable. And, of course, my concern throughout is that we come to rely on too few of these patterns. Parsimonious individuals are not handicapped by an inability to acquire new concepts. They are handicapped by overbearing inclinations and inhibitions against novelty in their use and development of plots.

In making out more clearly this plot notion of conceptualization, consider that plot use as a capacity has as a built-in

consequence of its productivity the tendency to become counterproductive. What makes economic use of response patterns
a productive strategy is that given a fairly stable environment,
that strategy allows and encourages *learning*; it makes experience productive in itself. But the tendency toward economy
of construal and response is paid for in declining flexibility and
inventiveness. That something has worked before becomes a
reason for its continued use. And there is further reinforcement
in that it is the agent's perceptions that determine success or
productivity. *Perceived* productivity suffices in a great many
instances. Even a disastrous course of action may be perceived
as successful by an agent, given special psychological conditions or needs. Short of simple nonsurvival, the agent will tailor
her or his success and failure just as he or she will tailor experience generally. The main job of plots is to cope with experience. But "coping" does not mean coping according to some
set of inviolable standards. If an individual fails to survive, we
may judge that he or she has failed to cope, but short of that
the judgement is a difficult one to make. Even a catatonic is
"coping". The difficulty in reaching him or her is precisely that
whatever the catatonic refuses to face is being "best" dealt with
by pathological withdrawal. Catatonic coping of course violates
de facto standards, the "norm", but these are ones *we* impose.
As long as plots work or are thought to work, they will continue
to be employed, and their working is not something that we
can determine and define ahistorically or even independently
of particular agents. We have an adaptive capacity that is guided
and governed by perception of success, and that perception is
itself in part guided and governed by plot use.

  Our environment is fairly stable. What we encounter is more
like what we have encountered than not, more often than not.
The most manifest indication of this is that we owe so much
to the experience of predecessors. We are record-keepers. We
value prior experience. Our libraries are full of prior experience, from "how to" books to abstract theory. It would seem
that the slow loss of flexible adaptability and the risk of counterproductive parsimony are fair enough prices to pay when
we consider the alternatives. The cost of a tendency toward
unfettered inventiveness might well be annihilation. Concep-

tualization, in being *ordering*, is inherently economical, is intrinsically parsimonious. To objectivize a world is to group, to pare, to relate and juxtapose in terms of (imposed or objective) similarity. That we do so initially in terms of how we act, not by intentional categorization, changes nothing. The objective still is to trim, to make what we encounter manageable.

But there is a tension here. Regardless of sentimentality, a hedgehog with one good trick is not as well off as a crafty fox with many. Among us, the people who do well are those whose ability to be flexible and inventive in dealing with the world is markedly above the norm. The problem this presents for me is basically the need to clarify what the empiricists never did fully deal with, namely, generalization. In other words, I must return to the matter mentioned earlier and say how it is that we employ plots in contexts other than those in which they first occur.

"Extracontextual" application of plots is conceived of as creativity or adaptive flexibility. From the perspective of my proposal it is actually the implementation of plots or parts of plots in widely varying circumstances. And the undeniable value of creativity and flexibility shows that parsimony is productive not only in enabling us to cope with experience but also in allowing us to go beyond past experience. What appears to be creativity is actually parsimony. Even though the employment of a construal or plot from one area in another area presents itself as genuinely new thinking with respect to the second area, it is parsimony in that a standing plot is employed to deal with a new situation (though "new situation" is used here in a third-person sense, since employment of a standing plot constitutes construal of the situation as *not* new in at least some crucial respects).

A brief article in the July 31, 1983, *New York Times* has it that metaphor is finally "getting its due" with respect to its influence on science: namely, recognition that scientific discovery involves often unrecognized reliance on analogy. Stephen Jay Gould is referred to as discussing the role of Darwin's understanding of "survival" in laissez-faire economics in his development of evolutionary theory. There is also reference to Roger S. Jones's characterization of Harvey's view of the heart as the center of circulation as related to Copernicus's heliocentric vision. There is even a somewhat strained point about noncausal physics owing something of its origins to cultural disorder in the Weimar Republic, to a Germanic abandonment of order at the subatomic level as prompted by the collapse of order at the social and political levels.

Certainly there is little to argue against the point that metaphors and analogies play a crucial conceptual role in perception and construal. But of interest to me is that to the extent that images and metaphors play the role in question, plot use begins to look less and less innovative. The novelty begins to shift from what looks like development of new plots to diverse application of standing plots. That is, our present picture is that we perceive analogies and then implement strategies or plots accordingly, so that it first occurs to a physicist that atomic particles are like suns and planets, and she or he can then pursue the parallel. This is too simple a picture. It is comparable to the old idea that a scientist goes about collecting "data" and then formulates a theory. But nothing is data except against the backdrop of a theory or a hypothesis or at least a problem. In like manner analogies do not just pop up, or if they do, they are often unfruitful. What is significant is perception of likeness in the context of a problem or situation. This is not to deny that metaphors and analogies are available in their own right, as it were. They are to be found in literature, in art, and so on. But the ones that count are those perceived by eyes looking for solutions, or at least with objectives. Dreaming of a snake with its tail in its mouth would prove productive only in the rarest of cases. But it proved highly productive in the case of a chemist puzzled about the molecular structure of benzene.

It was parsimonious to construe selection and survival in nature as one does success in the marketplace, and the result was an incredibly powerful theory about evolution. (It is striking that that theory then is applicable to better understanding success in the market.) As pointed out earlier, creativity is not a matter of the production of ideas out of nothing. Interpretive parsimony is actually what underlies a great deal of what we deem novel. This is evident even in art, where creativity is most sacrosanct. Art historians are not just spinning arcane notions when they trace artistic inspiration. We must understand that application of a standing plot in a context other than that of its initial application is probably the most common sort of creativity we are capable of. It is a very rare thing to introduce new perspectives or ideas. And as we saw earlier, this is not to denigrate our creativity. It is to be realistic about ourselves, and what we encounter, and what we add to the world. Stories such as the one about Newton and the falling apple are favorites of ours, and they are conceived of as stories about the merest prompting of genius. But the prompting of genius and genius itself require very complex backgrounds. There is little genius if any, without experience. And to the extent to which experience is a necessary condition of innovation, standing plots are necessary to innovation.

The tension between parsimony and the premium we put on creativity and flexibility, then, is more apparent than real. But what is a real enough problem for me is the shift in question: how a plot goes from implementation in one context to implementation in another. This is what passes for generalization. What we have are agents employing construals and behavioural patterns developed in one type of situation in types that diverge from the original.

As I have indicated, at some level what we do "just happens"; at another level we do again what we found effective, regardless of the nature of its initiation. But at still another level we act reflectively on the basis of experience. And at this level we do not simply repeat ourselves; we innovate. That our innovations use standing plots is, as we saw above, not of major interest. What is important here is that plots or parts of plots are taken out of one context and used in another. How does this occur, and why some and not others? Anyone with an interest in machine intelligence will recognize the issue about how programs might be overridden and extended in unforeseeable ways. It is something like when actors improvise, when they depart from their lines. It is novelty that poses the problem. That the novelty is not wholly creative is immaterial. It suffices that suddenly a tool is used to do something it was not designed to do.

Nor can I simply shift the burden to reflection. With regard to machine intelligence many would argue that what computers lack, the capacity we so jealously keep to ourselves, is reflection on experience. But not all novelty of construal and behaviour is reflective. We do not have a tidy two-tiered situation, where reflex suffices to a point beyond which reflection takes over (though admittedly this is the common view).

The view I have been sketching does not require intrinsic relevance of action to situation. I need only that action occur in a certain plenitude and that some prove productive. Later action is directed, but that is another story. As initial behaviour need not be specially keyed to objective situations faced, whatever those might be, so too plot adaption need not be specially keyed. We must stop thinking that all plot adaptation is intentional, that it presupposes perception of objective analogies or similarities. At least sometimes the "perception" of an analogy will be simply application of a plot. The *New York Times* article referred to above stresses that the analogies it mentions were invariably either denied or ignored by the creative scientists in question. Darwin might very well have been quite skeptical if told that his insights into survival of the fittest were shaped or made possible by his understanding of prospering in nineteenth-century markets. Not only can we not shift the burden of novelty to reflection, but it would seem that the interesting cases are mostly nonreflective. We may well find it enlightening to think that a physicist immersed in sociopolitical chaos is likelier to entertain notions about random events at the atomic level, but the physicist would probably resent the idea.

For every Darwin there are countless persons who extended plot use unproductively. Productive plot use is itself naturally selectable. Once this is appreciated it is easier to abandon the notion that innovative plot use is intentional, that the shift from one context to another is a deliberate one. We need to move away from the notion of perception of analogy to one of plot imposition.

What I want to suggest is that perception of analogies is not at all what we should focus on. Rather what we must consider is, again, just the productivity of behaviour. But it appears that in explaining innovative plot use I must make cleverness and genius just luck. It sounds as if some people are lucky in that their construals and behaviour in one area are also productive in another, while most find this not the case. It would then be a problem for me that some *consistently* benefit from multiple application of standing plots.

I think the key to understanding innovation is "thematic apperception". This psychological concept designates the manner in which we pick out of complex backgrounds items that interest us or are related to what interests us. Nor is this apperception intentional. While clearly a cognitive capacity, it is not a directed one. Given interests and goals, some things assume a special prominence. If these are features of objects or situations, they may prompt productive connections. The prominence of these items is not "objective"; it is a function of what we are up to at the time, as well as of our general interests and inclinations. The actual bases of the productive connections usually escape us and are normally postulated as earlier associations. (If psychologists cannot supply an abundance of examples, Proust can.)

Plot implementation must be guided by such "apperception". Something about a situation prompts reenactment or partial reenactment of a plot because of association with something about or in the context of original enactment. The result is application of the plot in question or some part of it in a new context. However, to do justice to our experience, my account must allow that inventive extracontextual implementation may involve hard thinking and striving for new ideas. From the agent's point of view, innovation usually will be experienced as an initial clear or vague perception of something in a new light, for instance, the evolving of species through natural selection of the fittest. But that perception may be preceded by effort, even if only of an undirected sort, and it will certainly be followed by effort at clarification and development. Nonetheless, the innovative perception is notoriously not an *intentional* product of deliberate effort. No amount of hard thinking necessarily leads directly to innovation as a product of deliberate effort. That is the point of genius. Otherwise inventive research would always be successful, given enough application.

To a degree thematic apperception explains innovative plot use only by moving the explanatory burden from innovation to its ground, perception or imposition of similarity or relatedness. But in my proposal there is, at some levels, no perception separate from plot use. Thematic apperception, then, is in some cases identical with innovative plot use. While at more advanced levels thematic apperception plays an explanatory role, at others it cannot explain plot use because it is coextensive with it. Where plot use is unreflective and cannot be distinguished from initial construal, "thematic apperception" only designates perception or imposition of similarity or relatedness. What underlies thematic apperception in these cases is below the intentional level. The operant associations or causal factors can only be postulated or perhaps got at to some extent through something like hypnosis. Here innovation is exhausted by plot implementation. It would be mistaken to look further for explanatory factors of an intentional sort. We would have to change the subject and look for *causes*. Therefore, while reflection will not explain innovation generally, it explains a crucial difference between innovation that is unreflective plot use or plot creation, and innovation that is a product of intentional effort.

Earlier it looked too much as if innovative plot use is happenchance. Thematic apperception is a helpful notion, but it does not change that basic picture. That is, the picture is of a great number of random applications of plots or construals beyond their contexts of origin and of a very few applications proving productive. This picture suggests that innovation and problem solving are accidental, that our efforts at invention and problem solving are basically random, and that innovation is exhausted by prior thought and action fortuitously implemented in new contexts. It appears that for inexplicable (causal) reasons or untraceable associations, a particular construal is applied beyond its original context. This seems simply insufficient to explain how we proceed in dealing with challenging situations and is why I have allowed that effort may result in innovation.

How in my proposed scheme, which construes thought and action in terms of plot use, can innovation be more than fortuitous extension or creation of plots?

Innovation emerges as important because it focuses the question of our experience of being thinkers and agents. After all, where innovation is wholly unreflective, it can be explained well enough in causal terms. It poses a problem precisely where it involves conscious effort. And in just these cases it is paradigmatic of mental activity that does not seem amenable to understanding in terms of narrative implementation or plot use. We have here something of a test case.

There is a crucial difference between, say, recalling a name and recalling how to deal with a situation or planning how to deal with a situation. Sometimes in the two latter cases the procedure may just come to us of a piece, but usually it will be a matter of recalling or envisaging steps coming in a certain order and each suggesting something about the next. An ancillary difference is that in the first case the effort is without real form; it is distinguished only by its objective. In a word, we simply do not know what it is we do when we try to recall a name. We strain at "having" the name, and when it occurs to us, we cannot say how or why, except perhaps to mention certain associations. In the case of recalling or devising a procedure, we work in a certain sequence, we envisage now this, now that maneuver, and so on, and we can say how we proceed.

The difference in question allows me to say that the problem of the apparent fortuitousness of innovation does not arise with respect to simple cases of something "coming to mind", no more than does our recalling a name require our knowing how we do so. This is not to say that I am making much of the simplicity of what comes to mind. A chess expert might recall a complicated defense as I do a name. The simplicity has to do with the mode of presentation or apprehension, not content. Against the simple cases are those where what comes to mind does so in a piecemeal manner and where there is discernible process. In these latter cases we speak of something being "thought out".

Where there is process, there is room for effort of a deliberate sort with respect to the way we make use of experience or of what cognitive psychologists call "domain specific" knowledge. Where such process is lacking, effort is directionless and perhaps even irrelevant to results. We can establish no reliable connection between effort and result, regardless of how conscious the effort. In these latter cases nothing is jeopardized by characterizing innovation as fortuitous, providing only that we acknowledge the necessary wherewithal, namely, the requisite "knowledge base".

Given process and reflection, there can be effective effort at juxtaposing and comparing, relating and hypothesizing. We can entertain possibilities and then select among them. We can test a chosen possibility, and so on. In this way we may be productively innovative, and talent and training play their full parts.

It is no part of my proposal to suggest that plot use is a matter of all human behaviour's being a determined acting out of so many scenarios. To suggest that would be to make narratives or plots *causes* of behaviour, when what I have tried to argue is that plots or narratives just are how we construe and respond to the world. I want only to insist on the possibility of repetition or reenactment not to attribute behaviour to plots working as causes.

To end this chapter I must further clarify a fundamental aspect of my proposal about narrative employment, one highlighted by the discussion of innovation.

The complexity and richness of human behaviour are assured by reflection and extensive experience. This complexity is most evident in the very fact that we do not recognize our behaviour to be patterned, except in special circumstances, as when our attention is drawn to a particular pattern. But in acknowledging complexity a matter arises that has haunted my proposal and is now unavoidable: If I accommodate the complexity evident in human behaviour, do I not seriously undermine the entire notion of a plot or narrative? I can accommodate complexity in one of two ways, by multiplying plots or by allowing plots to be very "open", to be mere sketches. The latter effectively empties the plot notion of content, but the former suggests that given any behaviour, *some* plot can be described as operant, and this seems to render the notion of a plot redundant, if not empty.

My embarrassment is that precisely because my proposal is a pragmatic one about construals, it does come to saying that we can always describe behaviour in terms of an operant plot.

Hence we do multiply plots to accommodate behaviour. I do not want to construe plots as too open or flexible because, while I may not want to claim certainty with respect to the roles of given plots, I do want it accepted that something is operant in behaviour that has a significant coherence.

The basic thrust of my narrative proposal is that the functional elements of human behaviour are not individual acts and thoughts, not "bits" of behaviour and cogitation. These are like letters or words, to return to the analogy used in discussing concepts. Such elements are too basic to support understanding of human behaviour, as letters and even words are insufficient for an understanding of discourse or natural language. The latter enterprise requires that sentences be taken as the functional elements. Likewise, if we want to understand human behaviour, and particularly attitudinal change, we must focus on elements that cohere as intelligible wholes. My proposal is that individual thoughts and acts are abstracted from composites that are comparable to the sentences of a language, coherent wholes that I have described as narratives or plots. To look beyond these, for my purposes, is like peering too closely at a newspaper photograph and having it dissolve into so many black dots.

But assuming plots as functional elements, can I countenance a plethora of plots in acknowledging the apparently infinite variety of human behaviour?

I want to avoid questions about identity criteria for plots, for while having postulated that these obtain as dispositional patterns available for implementation, I do not want to bog down in a thoroughly nonpragmatic discussion of how we count plots. But I do seem to have an embarrassment of riches in too many possible plots. This embarrassment dissipates, though, in considering that the focal point of the discussion is not complexity of thought and action but its lack, in realizing that the explanatory value of my narrative proposal has to do with *restriction*, with individuals coming to think and behave in limited ways. If human behaviour were always diverse and (reasonably) novel, then the notion of a plot or narrative would be redundant in that there would be too many ascribable plots for the notion to be useful. But as we age, we precisely seem to move from broad behavioural and attitudinal repertories to narrower ones.

Talk of plots and narratives would still prove of value even if restricted to simple behaviour and to understanding how we initially build up repertories of thought and action. But it would lose both productiveness and plausibility when applied to advanced reflective thought and action, were it not precisely that these seem to grow restricted with age. This is what we need to understand, and it is why plot or narrative talk is useful. Plot employment may well be rendered unattributable by behavioural complexity, and its discussion be unproductive where there is flexibility of construal and response. But it becomes attributable and its discussion productive in those cases where behaviour has become worryingly inflexible and construals are obtrusively rigid.

The acknowledgement of the complexity and openness of human behaviour actually is less a problem than a limitation on our questioning. The point can be illustrated with an analogy. When authorities deny that radioactive exposure poses a health hazard, what they mean is that no direct link can be established between the exposure and, say, consequent cancers in the population. In other words, they mean something like "does not pose an *establishable* health hazard." Causes of ill effects fall below the level at which we can say that an increase in cancer cases is due to that exposure. No responsibility can be assigned, because causal links cannot be traced and harmful influences cannot be identified. But this in no way negates whatever effect the exposure may have. That effect is real enough, even if untraceable. In like manner a plot may be operant even if we cannot identify with certainty what determinants are operant in someone's behaviour. And this limitation applies to the individual agent too. This is a pragmatic point. We cannot productively contend that just this or that motive or plot is at work in a given case, even in our own behaviour. We may postulate, as when we say that social and political chaos prompted serious consideration by some physicist of random events at the subatomic level. The idea may be useful, but it is not *right* or *wrong*. And this is so regardless of what the physicist thinks or says.

The analogy brings out that speaking of an operant plot is proffering a construal. It is a way of seeing certain behaviour. We are not able to pursue the matter to establish that the construal is *correct* in the sense of constituting an accurate description of objective processes. When we speak of plot use, or more commonly of motivation or perception, we propose construals; we do not articulate discoveries or discernments. Plausibility and productivity are the only standards to be met, and these represent no more than present consensus. The closest we come to actual description is in pathological cases, where we describe what underlies compulsive, rigidly determined behaviour. In these cases, talk of compelling, mechanistic implementation of well-defined plots approaches accurate description. But basically we trade in interpretations, not descriptions. The initially embarrassing multitude of plots indicates not that human behaviour is in fact infinitely variable, and the result of continuous free will, but rather that any description of it at a certain level of complexity must always be interpretive. The plethora of plots is not metaphysical excess but recognition of complexity and a certain indeterminacy inherent in human motivation.

Here we touch on what was said earlier about hermeneutics. My problem is essentially one of what may be understood by speaking of plot use. And my options are just those represented by Emilio Betti and Hans-Georg Gadamer in philosophical hermeneutics. On one hand is Betti's view that hermeneutical interpretation is directed on discernment, on "re-cognition" of objective meaningfulness; on the other is Gadamer's view that interpretation is itself constitutive of what is understood. I follow Gadamer and reject the possibility of correct interpretation, of accurate understanding. Interpretation is always just that and can never amount to objective discernment. In Betti's view it is at least possible to believe that one is approaching correct understanding of original intention and thought, assuming one can further believe that such thought and intention had the necessary degree of determinacy. In like manner some would expect that motivation and most aspects of conceptualization should be in principle discernible and that abandonment of this assumption would render human behaviour inexplicable. But there simply is no possibility of correct discernment of what produces a given piece of behaviour. The only argument required to support this point is the observation that we manifestly lack criteria for establishing correctness. What we strive for, even in theoretical explanation, is consistency and plausibility. And of course these are always geared to standards we impose.

Much of the material in this and previous chapters has been rather abstract. It was necessary to provide a basis on which to ground characterization of interpretive parsimony of a more practical sort. That basis consists of my proposal about narrative employment and the development of some aspects of that proposal, particularly how plot use is patterned conceptualization that nonetheless allows for the complexity and innovativeness of human behaviour. If my proposal has been made out more or less plausibly, I must now turn to a more focused consideration of interpretive parsimony. Parsimony is coming to do too little in coping with experience; it is coming to rely on too few construals of, and responses to, what we encounter. In the next chapter I shall consider some of the more important aspects of parsimony, with a view to giving a fuller picture of how perspective changes that may accompany aging can best be understood.

5

The Aspects of Parsimony

Interpretive parsimony is not, of course, as simple as my remarks so far may suggest. Thus far I have concentrated on the dispositional and behavioural aspects. Doing so was necessary because my proposal about narrative employment must initially be made out in terms of responsive behaviour. I must now look at the categorical, as opposed to dispositional, aspect of parsimony. That is, I must consider how narrative employment and parsimony operate in connection with states of consciousness we attribute without direct reference to behaviour.

In the preceding chapters I focused on inclinations to respond to the world in various ways. These construals of the world, both of the sort identical with behaviour and more reflective kinds, were described fairly simply. But with experience and reflective awareness construals grow complex and gain another dimension. Individuals soon begin to anticipate, to categorize reflectively. This involves acquiring and having certain "pictures" of how the world is and how it will continue to be. These pictures encompass more than one or another individual construal. They come to have the status of broad construals that serve as contexts for more specific and particular ones. They are like standing plots of a very wide and flexible sort, covering quite diverse behaviour. They are made possible by reflection and are reinforced by experience that particular responses are more effective if guided by general principles.

We can best think of these pictures as plots generalized by repeated implementation in many disparate circumstances. They then come to dictate broadly the shape of perception and behaviour in being enacted in many diverse situations. It is these general determinants of thought and action that we attribute as attitudes and conceive of as detachable from any given behaviour. And we erroneously think of these as causes of behaviour. But what makes these attitudes only *like* standing plots is that they are attributed categorically, both as operant in the determination of behaviour over time *and* as attitudes reflectively experienced by those to whom they are attributed. They are persisting states of their subjects in being experienced, as opposed to being manifest only in periodic behaviour. At an unreflective level plots suffice. But at a reflective level there must be very general construals not exhausted by behaviour and narrowly focused self-consciousness. The categorical aspect of dealing with experience is the conscious having of attitudes.

It is this categorical aspect of parsimony that is most recognizable to us, for it is in the recognition of attitudes, in the sense of reflectively experiencing them, that we are most conscious of the internal determinants of our thought and action. The point is nicely illustrated by how we fit the parsimonious into our pictures of the world. We do not, of course, recognize that fitting as parsimony on our own parts, but that is what it is. We deal with those much older than ourselves by consciously thinking them possessed of restrictive attitudes. We cope with them, as part of our experience, by attributing to them attitudes as restrictive as we take up just in coping with them. In this way they become a manageable part of our lives. It is easier so to proceed than to treat each as an individual. Of course we do the same with the not-so-old and the young, whom we group in various ways, but it is how we deal with older people that is most relevant here. And it is this conscious attitude toward the old that must first be changed. An understanding of interpretive parsimony should facilitate deliberate modification of this attitude.

Our perception of the elderly centers on how we think they experience the world. Though we do not now call it that, we attribute extreme interpretive parsimony of a categorical as well as dispositional sort to the elderly. We anticipate restrictions on older people in terms of physical limitations, but more importantly, we anticipate narrowness, disinterest, or vagueness in attention, not only in terms of how they behave but in how they *think*. We constantly adjust what we say to those significantly older than ourselves, as well as what we do that involves them. We intellectually slow our pace, as when we slow our steps so as not to exert a companion. But with the old we are prompted to do so less by indications that they are failing to keep up than because of assumptions that they cannot keep up.

These assumptions concerning the elderly are self-confirming to a deplorable degree, for they determine not only our initial view of someone older but also our construals of whatever they may do or say. Moreover, these assumptions impose restrictions not only on their objects but also on those who hold them, both in terms of immediate activity that involves older people and, in time, in terms of their own activities. Furthermore, these assumptions are not only self-confirming in perception, but they are self-confirming in effect. Few people realize that how they treat others to some extent determines what those others become, how they come to be treated by still others and, eventually, by themselves. (Recall here Cowley's remark quoted in the preface.)

The overall effects of assumptions about older people go well beyond the distress of the individuals who are their targets. My mother, who at seventy-six has been involved for some eight years with the Foster Grandparents Plan and who has found great satisfaction in the program, complains that what is most difficult for her is working with the younger participants in the plan, such as social workers.[1] For too many of these younger workers, the volunteer grandparents are as much charges as the young children they are all trying to help. And the key factor in the attitude of the younger workers seems to be their expectations about the older volunteers' interests and abilities. Of course professional training is a factor in the attitudes in question, but it seems to be a less dominant one than the mere assumption of restricted interest and awareness.

In the case of the Foster Grandparents Plan, effectiveness on the part of the adult group toward the subject group, the children in need, is clearly jeopardized by division within the adult group. If some members of the adult group deal with other members of that group as if the latter are a separate subject group, or even part of the basic subject group, then clearly cooperation among the adults will be considerably less than ideal. And there will be ancillary difficulties, such as awareness on the part of the children of dissent among those on whom they are dependent.

The foster grandparent is cast as a charge in the plots of the younger social workers in virtue of stereotypic views of older people, though possibly also because of personal experience. But the result is that the older workers are not perceived as *fellow* workers by the younger ones. At best individual contributions may be acknowledged, and perhaps only grudgingly ("She's not bad with the kids, for someone her age"). There is, then, not only the individual, personal cost of present attitudes toward older people but also the institutional cost of decreased effectiveness. And there is additional consequential personal cost, for eventually the younger person will assign at least parts of the stereotypes to himself or herself as he or she ages. The stereotyping may come to be partly understood, and resented, but many of the basic attitudes will remain operant. And in being operant, they will not only inhibit the individual, but they will make him or her conform to the stereotypic expectations of his or her own juniors. The younger person adopts attitudes that not only bar effective cooperation with older people, such as the foster grandparents, but eventually restrict her or his own effectiveness and participation in all sorts of activities. At some time the person will see himself or herself as he or she saw the grandparents much earlier.

The foster grandparent case illustrates the duality of stereotypic attitudes about the aged. There is the side in which others are perceived in light of certain expectations, and there is the side in which one perceives or comes to perceive oneself in light of those same expectations. At one stage the attitudes determine how others are treated, at another they determine how one thinks and feels and acts. But while this duality is fairly clear, what is perhaps less clear is the duality with which we began this chapter and which underlies the other, namely, that of the dispositional and the categorical.

One can look at the attitudes at issue here from two perspectives. On one hand they can be dealt with as I have been doing, in terms of behaviour or the implementation of standing plots. On the other hand the attitudes can be ascribed to an individual in a categorical way. To admit this is to acknowledge what classical behaviourism could not: that we must talk about *both* dispositions and persisting states of mind. We cannot understand parsimony if we restrict ourselves to the dispositional and fail to understand it in terms of advanced reflective states of mind, in terms of how things look to individuals in light of their experience and their years of coping. The reason is that when standing plots begin to coalesce and form broader patterns, to constitute attitudes available to reflection, they become persisting states of mind that are separate from their particular enactments and are experienced by their subjects *as* attitudes. Talk of plot use eventually leads us to recognition and discussion of the way that standing plots come to constitute determinants of behaviour that are categorically attributable states as opposed to dispositionally attributable behaviour patterns.

The categorical/dispositional duality raises some old philosophical problems. Dispositional analyses of mind, such as Rylean behaviourism, were reductive in being attempts to dispense with categorically attributable states. The latter pose difficulties because of questions about their nature "in the order of being". Some insist on construing them as irreducibly mental and others as identifiable with states of the brain. There are also questions about whether such states, regardless of their nature, are causes of behaviour or the wherewithal for the exercise of free will. Recent functionalist views, such as that of Jerry Fodor, have defused these difficulties in the view of many, but the traditionally inclined will see talk of categorically attributable states as involving commitments of a metaphysical sort.[2] At least such attribution will be taken as precluding physicalism and behaviourism. From the pragmatic point of view these are sterile debates and irresoluble because of the nature of their presuppositions. In any case, I do not wish to reduce consciousness to behaviour or plot use, nor do I wish to milk metaphysical import from the admission that we enjoy conscious states.

What I want to do is integrate talk of plot use with more familiar categorical attitude attribution. My narrative-employment proposal has it that parsimony is a matter of restricted plot use and plot creation. How are categorically attributable states to be understood in terms of this proposal? I have suggested that repeated use of plots may result in patterns that can be identified with attitudes. But this takes me only a little way. I need to spell out how categorical attitude ascription can be squared with plot use terminology.

As noted, my proposal is not a reductivist one, for there is no intention of analyzing away attitudes in terms of implemented and standing plots. There can be a reductive proposal only where the reality of the object phenomenon is essentially denied. It is no part of my proposal to deny the reality of attitudes as persisting, categorically attributable states. My thesis is not a metaphysical one. I am concerned with manners of speaking, with construals. My proposal is functionalist in that it is directed toward understanding perspective narrowing in terms of plots *whatever* these may be thought to be "in the order of being". What I need to do is take attitudes into account and understand their relation to plots, but not thereby reduce them to plots. It is not that attitudes are "nothing more" than plots; rather it is that we can best understand attitudes, at least of a certain sort, if we speak of them in terms of plots and their implementation. My problem, then, is integrating two ways of speaking, not establishing the existence or nonexistence of anything.

However, worries about "the order of being" persist, for plot talk is at odds with attitude talk to the extent that the former does not tolerate attribution of persistence in a way that the latter requires. While plots may be standing plots and be available for use, they are not as such intentional items. This is to say that standing plots are not conscious mental states in being available for use, though their content may be envisaged. But attitudes are at least sometimes intentional. They are capable of being *conscious* attitudes, even when nothing is being done. I cannot simply reconceive attitudes as dispositional and dismiss their persistence, for that would be to argue a reductive thesis. We think of people as simply having certain attitudes quite independently of saying or doing anything. Of course we also think of someone being able to speak a second language even though they are not doing so at the moment and may not have done so for some time, but this is clearly a dispositional property. A person is not, as it were, in a French or Spanish state of mind while chatting in English, though we may say so (precisely!) to characterize his or her attitude. Feeling hostile toward someone is not necessarily just doing and saying hostile things. One may seethe with resentment even though outwardly placid. At the very least, this is what we think, and we are dubious about Rylean claims that attitudes really are dispositional properties and would be seen to be such if we could free ourselves from the grip of Cartesian dualism.

I have to leave room for something of an attitudinal nature that can persist in the sense of being a state of mind even though the subject in question is not engaging in any behaviour. But this point is different from the point made by people such as D. M. Armstrong against Gilbert Ryle.[3] The point here is not that dispositional explanations are empty unless dispositional behaviour can be attributed to underlying, persisting states. For one thing, Armstrong finds the sorts of attitudes I am discussing as embarrassing as Ryle did. He cannot offer a materialistic analysis of such states because they are persisting *conscious* states; hence, his own attempts to reduce them.

Being ill disposed toward a student whose work is regularly late is something that is continuous for at least periods of time in a way that speaking to or complaining about the student is not. The latter is episodic as plot use is episodic, while the former is how someone feels over certain periods of time. When we consider more general attitudes, such as expecting that older persons will be forgetful and inattentive, we seem to be closer to continuous attitudes or feelings than to something episodic, even though dispositional accounts of these attitudes will sometimes suffice. And what seems clear is that what my description of plot use neglects is just the experience of having a certain attitude over and above doing what we do.

At least some of the time we are reflexively aware of something best described as underlying our behaviour, as opposed to being identical with our behaviour. It would seem, then, that plot use, if only in more advanced cases, proceeds from and requires persisting states capable of being conscious even if not always so. The difficulty for my proposal is that it now looks as if narrative employment will prove useful for understanding only the *manifestation* of attitudes. But I want it to serve for understanding attitudes themselves, if only to the extent of understanding their fixity and paucity under certain conditions. My problem comes to this: If I cannot integrate plot talk and attitude talk, I will have to accept attitudes as primary givens and as not explicable in terms of plots with respect to their acquisition, retention, and employment. Plot talk would then be restricted to the manifestation of attitudes, and my proposal would lose most of its force and leave attitudes no better understood than they now are.

As I have outlined, the kernel of my difficulty is that attitudes are (sometimes) had in the sense of being experienced as ongoing and distinct from their behavioural manifestations. It looks as if for my narrative proposal to work, I should say how all cases of such experienced attitudes are really cases of plot implementation. But that is, in effect, behaviourism; it is to argue that all categorically attributable mental states are instances of overt or covert behaviour. Not only is this a reductivist thesis, but it is one that has never been made out and that clashes with experience. It might well be that argument could lead us to construe our experience differently, to become Ryleans, but that seems rather too faint a hope, assuming it to be a desirable objective.

We experience acting on the basis of our attitudes and hence cannot accept that having attitudes just is acting in some way. Plot talk leaves no room for this experience, and, reciprocally, attitude talk seems to downgrade plot talk seriously to being about the consequences of attitudes.

The having of an attitude is much vaguer than the having

of an emotion or a feeling, yet the latter is often equated with the former. For instance, we gloss regularly having a given feeling as having an attitude. Generally feeling resentful of those more fortunate, for example, is described as being an envious or grudging person: that is, a person with a certain persisting attitude. On the other hand, ascription of attitudes often does not involve ascriptions of feelings. When we speak of broad perspectives, we tend to refer to attitudes without amplification ("I just don't like her attitude").

The American Heritage Dictionary defines "attitude" in three ways: as a posture or manner; as a state of mind or feeling; and as an object's orientation in space. The first and third interest me only insofar as their etymologies are suggestive. What is interesting about the second is the facility with which the term "feeling" is used. A "feeling" is in turn defined as either a sensation or an affective state, emotion, or disposition. It is also defined as an awareness or impression and as an opinion, a sensibility or, again, an attitude. Short of theoretical definitions, it is clear that "attitude" and "feeling" are very open and flexible terms, relying for their effectiveness on context and intuitive uptake. They designate roughly how things are for someone. What is also clear is the presumption of intentionality, the assumption that these are states of mind which we consciously have. In fact, it sounds a little odd to speak of attitudes otherwise ("He has real antipathy for academics but does not realize it"). Such usage suggests self-deception, special aspect blindness, or rationalization.

It seems safe to say that in common usage speaking of attitudes is largely speaking of how individuals feel on a regular basis. Feeling hostile on one or another occasion is one thing, feeling hostile a good deal of the time is being belligerent, having a belligerent attitude. Here is where Ryle's arguments found some support, for if we focus on attitudes, it does seem that dispositional accounts will suffice. It is when we speak of how a belligerent person feels at a particular time that we need to attribute mental states categorically. (Again, we are not here concerned with Armstrong's point about the grounds of dispositional behaviour but with what it is like to *feel* hostile.)

I might sum up by saying that it is the periodic "self-luminescence" of attitudes as experienced feelings that poses a problem by escaping the net of plot use and creation. With respect to aging, the self-luminescence of attitudes does not affect attitudes' growing fewer and more restricted. Self-perception notoriously need not yield anything at odds with expectations. But this luminescence is relevant in another way. If having an attitude is at least sometimes having it in a conscious manner over a period of time, that will not change with age. It will be an inherent characteristic of attitudes, if one at all. Some awareness of having fewer and/or more restricted attitudes can be expected, then, given reasonable memory, whereas if attitudes were reducible to behaviour, parsimony would likely be evident only to others. The awareness in question seems manifest in the justificatory and apologetic things older people say about no longer being interested in something, no longer thinking something important, and even in expressions of what is taken as greater tolerance. These expressions largely explain one or another sort of disengagement from some aspect of intellectual or social activity ("I don't read much anymore; I can't seem to find anything interesting"; "I don't follow politics anymore; all the candidates seem the same"; "I can't be bothered with international disputes anymore; each side has its points").

The interpretation or rationalization of parsimony takes the direction I mentioned in the introduction. Change is attributed to deeper understanding, greater experience, and sophistication ("When you're my age, you realize that . . . "). If there is recognition of increased restriction or parsimony, the blame is put on the world, not oneself. It is deemed that people are, after all, not so complex or that simple principles underly everything. Only occasionally will there be concern that the fault is in oneself, that something is being missed. The last is a concern of the young who need to worry about what is beyond their experience simply because their experience repeatedly proves inadequate. The parsimonious are precisely convinced that there is no call for more than the construals that they already have and that have as repeatedly proven adequate.

The line I want to take in dealing with categorically attributable states is that attitude talk, when not dispositional, is talk about recurrent feelings. Even if this is unsatisfactory as a general description, it covers just those cases which most concern me, namely, instances of attitudes experienced *as* attitudes.

My first observation is that there are only two options with respect to self-knowledge of categorically attributed states in general and attitudes in particular. Either there is occasional reflexive awareness of dispositions as perspectives or attitudes, or there is inductive awareness achieved through third parties or inferences from consideration of one's own behaviour ("Perhaps I *am* prejudiced, I always seem to . . . "). My second observation is that attitudes are not simply had or not had, as one might or might not have a physical property. Their attribution, even to oneself, is a matter of putting a certain construction on thought and behaviour. One man's aggressiveness is another's assertiveness. There are broad, culturally defined limits and guidelines for attribution of attitudes and of course the conventional meanings of attitude terms, but the first are very flexible in particular cases and the second open-textured. That is to say, there are no definite criteria for application of attitude terms.

The preceding observations are at odds with one another because the ambiguity acknowledged by the second is denied by the first's conception of reflexive awareness of feelings as direct and possibly incorrigible. Ambiguities attaching to identification and attribution of attitudes in third-person cases should be acknowledged as extending to first-person cases. But many think the first-person case a privileged one because identification and attribution are seen as "immediate" in reflexive awareness of attitudes or feelings. The putative directness or immediacy is taken as precluding that the attitudes or feelings in question could be anything but exactly as experienced. Against this view, it would seem that I must dissolve feelings and attitudes in an acid-bath of plot use, leaving nothing but behaviour to serve as the object of possible direct awareness. It will look as if I cannot protect the centrality of plot talk if

I tolerate references to persisting mental states that are in no way identifiable with narrative employment because directly experienced as this or that feeling. I think the error is to think that feelings must be independent of and prior to plot use in some holistic way. The common view is that we must allow for instances of reflexive awareness of attitudes as inviolate and primary experiential phenomena. This is just the old empiricist mistake of thinking reflexive awareness elementally simple and incorrigible by ignoring the role of conceptualization in even the most elementary case of awareness. Of course, if feelings were holistically independent of and prior to plot use, they would, by their very existence and attribution, relegate plot talk to being about their consequences. But feelings constitutively involve conceptualization; they are themselves products of conceptualization. They are not the pure givens of classical empiricism. Feelings are decidedly not independent of or prior to plot use and are not holistic because they are not simple.

Awareness occurs within operant plots, from within implemented narratives. Plots mold consciousness; they do not follow it. Of course some plots are more basic than others. Some allow a good deal of reflection, while others are the ground of reflection. But we experience having an attitude or a feeling within an operant plot. To be hostilely disposed toward a person or group, for instance, is to be implementing a narrative. It is within that narrative that a person or a group has the qualities that are the focus of the hostility. And to be hostile we must ourselves have a place in the narrative. It may not be too much to say that we formulate such concepts as that of hostility on the basis of familiarity with plots.[4]

We must distinguish between a feeling or reflexive awareness of an attitude as a state of consciousness and the object or content of that state, namely, what that state is consciousness of. States of consciousness as such are prior to plot use or narrative implementation, but their content is not. To the extent that we can, in the abstract, speak of consciousness in itself we are speaking of what precedes narrative implementation. Mine is not a behaviourist or reductivist proposal in which being conscious reduces to implementing narratives. But the contents of states of consciousness are determined by plots precisely to the extent that those contents are conceptualized. The identification I am arguing for is not between being conscious and implementing narratives but between conceptualization and plot use or creation. Once this is seen, it should be clear that reference to persisting, categorically attributable states poses no special difficulty, so long as the contents of those states are acknowledged to be shaped by narrative.

Once the difference between a state of consciousness and its content is appreciated, we see that attribution of feelings—that is, of attitudes reflexively experienced—involves two aspects. I must be careful to avoid the error that haunts philosophy, namely, the introduction of ad hoc devices such as the empiricists' unconscious inferences and Russell's tacit existential assertions, but attribution of a feeling clearly does include both categorical attribution of consciousness and attribution of content, as all intentional states have objects. We seldom concern ourselves with this difference, because our interest is in the content of these states; we take consciousness as such for granted in attributing attitudes. But the difference does surface at times, as when we are speaking of someone who is unaware of his or her attitudes. Our attributions have to do with how someone is disposed toward something. This is in part to say how they *feel*, given self-awareness of the attitude, but it is also to say how the objects of the attitude are construed. The best evidence of the distinction is that the quickest way to change an attitude is to inform its bearer that the object in question has been misidentified in some way.

I need to integrate plot talk and attitude talk, or that part of the latter that involves categorical attribution. I can begin to do so by observing that even where attitude talk is categorical, plot talk is applicable with respect to characterization of the objects of the attitudes we ascribe categorically. It then emerges how attributed attitudes are feelings when categorically ascribed, for it is at those times that an attitude's objects are consciously apprehended in a particular way by the bearer of the attitudes. My concern was that acknowledgement of categorical attribution might leave me with states that were prior to and independent of narrative implementation. But there is no real difficulty, for categorical attribution of attitudes none-theless requires explication of the conceptualization of the objects of the attributed attitudes, and it is with respect to conceptualization that plot talk plays its unique role.

One reason that categorical attribution appears so important is that, as noted, we tend to think of attitudes as states of mind that are *causes* of behaviour. Categorical attribution, then, seems necessary in order to accommodate what we think explains dispositional behaviour by being its cause. But this is to confuse categorical attribution with the point referred to earlier as argued by Armstrong against Ryle. The problem is not the causes of dispositional behaviour. A theoretical answer to that question will likely involve attribution of persisting, underlying states that are the causes of dispositional behaviour, but are not self-conscious states. Armstrong seems quite right in saying against Ryle's "phenomenalist" conception of dispositions that without such underlying states dispositional explanation is no explanation at all, for it is only the attribution of inexplicable periodic behaviour. Against this, my concern is with how when we describe someone as, say, belligerent, we sometimes mean they *feel* belligerent, not just that they say and do belligerent things. Categorical attribution is necessary to describe how the world is for someone over time, even if only periodically. It is easy to confuse this with describing causes of behaviour, because to say how the world is for someone is to speak of persisting states of consciousness, and these seem ideally suited to be the causes of behaviour. But these persisting states are at least not the sole causes of behaviour. For one thing, we sometimes engage in behaviour not preceded by such states. For another, these states are compatible with behaviour at odds with themselves. We often surprise ourselves, for instance, by answering politely when consumed with resentment. We may think ourselves intimidated or angry but behave other than in strict conformity with how we feel. Whatever the causes of behaviour, they are not necessarily identical with our self-conscious states. If these were the causes of behaviour, then my narrative proposal would face difficulties, for, as I have said, it would be confined to the consequences of categorically attributed states. If so limited, the proposal would be only a way of speaking about what follows conceptualization and attitudes, and not about conceptualization and attitudes themselves. As it is, I need only to acknowledge categorically attributed states, keeping in mind that as intentional states they will constitutively involve conceptualization. That means plot talk is applicable to the description of the contents of those states. The integration of plot talk and attitude talk requires only recognition of their diverse applications. Both are about how things are for the subject; but while attitude talk does little more than say that things are thus and so, plot talk allows us to say a good deal about *how* they are thus and so. And that is of primary interest to us in the present enterprise.

Categorical attribution of attitudes might be glossed as our saying how the world is for someone on occasions when the subject is conscious of the world in the way in question. Dispositional attribution concerns how someone has acted, may be acting, and will likely act. Dispositional attribution almost certainly carries implications about persisting, underlying causal states that explain why individuals act as they do and that are themselves attributed categorically. But these causal states are not necessarily identical with those we attribute categorically as self-conscious. We tend to think they are, but that is because we confuse feelings with causes of behaviour. We tend to see what an agent does as a direct consequence of her or his self-conscious states. But this tendency does not allow for the complexity of motivational and causal processes underlying behaviour. Nor does it allow for the fact that some of our states of consciousness may be as they are precisely because we are going to act or are acting in a way at odds with related states, as in the case of rationalized behaviour.

Confusing self-conscious states with causes of behaviour is one of the things that results in too simplistic a view of human thought and behaviour, for it leads us to think of these states as the *only* causes of behaviour. Our traditional picture is a thoroughly Cartesian one in which there is an inner theater where self-conscious ideas occur, and there is overt behaviour, which is the outcome of those occurrences. We are not prepared to consider that some self-conscious states are themselves *effects*, quite possibly of the same causes responsible for our behaviour. When we allow nonselfconscious factors to count as influencing behaviour, we think in vague terms of something having gone amiss, of some extraneous force having interfered with normal processes. We think of such things as subconscious desires, pathological inclinations, and even posthypnotic suggestion.

I have suggested that categorical attribution is attribution of dispositions as they are experienced by their subjects. The importance of this to my proposal about narrative employment is that categorically attributed states do not escape the net of plot talk. Their content remains addressable in terms of plot use and plot creation. Whatever we may say about self-consciousness, the content of such states must be conceptualized, so that one is self-conscious of just this or that. And it is in determining that content that plots are operant.

But how does what I have said help us to understand parsimony?

Consideration of the main aspects of parsimony, the dispositional and categorical, helps us to understand how plot use or construal appears to the subject at some times. That is, given the imposition of narratives that organize the subject's experience, that subject will sometimes enjoy reflexive or self-conscious awareness of his or her construals. This will invariably occur at fairly high levels of conceptual complexity, but it does occur. Moreover, in acknowledging self-consciousness, we acknowledge that being conscious is, in itself, something that precedes plot use. But that it does has little bearing on my proposal, for consciousness so considered is only a necessary condition of plot use or narrative implementation. Consciousness as such is "empty"; it must be filled with objects of consciousness, however simple or complex these may be. Plots are operant in the shaping of that content.

Consideration of the main aspects of parsimony also clears the way for discussion of some secondary aspects. One of these is an increase in lack of communicative effectiveness. This is an increasing failure on the part of the parsimonious to convey clearly how they feel and what they are thinking because of a narrowing of receptivity to others. As they grow more restricted in their ability to respond to others, the parsimonious grow less able to communicate with them because they become more prone to address others in inappropriate ways. This failure is compounded by stereotypic expectations on the part of others, because communicative ineptness tends to confirm those expectations. The parsimonious vitiate their communicative efforts mainly by addressing persons of their own making, persons truncated by narrowed perception. And those so misaddressed will likely perceive communicative failure as due to the age of the parsimonious individual.

Communicative difficulties may make the parsimonious individual wonder if he or she might not be missing something, but such wonderment is usually unproductive. For it to lead to resolution of the difficulties that prompt it, the parsimonious individual must become less parsimonious. He or she must come to perceive interlocutors very differently and recognize as meaningful what is otherwise wholly misperceived or not perceived at all. For example, in order not to misaddress a much younger person in a particular context, the parsimonious individual may have to suspend judgments about the propriety of, say, street demonstrations; he or she may have to consider that activity as meaningful political expression as opposed to either youthful excess (for the liberal) or mob rule (for the conservative). Literature is full of stories that turn on a parent's painful reassessment of a son's or daughter's values. But the parsimonious individual faces communicative failure with *most* people, not only family members, and in most areas of interaction.

Communicative failure is an aspect of parsimony, as opposed to being a product of it, because of the manner in which such failure contributes to and reinforces parsimony. Not only does communicative failure confirm the expectations of others about the general incompetence of the overly parsimonious, but it both entrenches the parsimonious practices responsible for the failure and reinforces related attitudes. For example, a parsimonious older person will be further convinced of indifference or even hostility on the part of the young when he or she fails to communicate with the young. And this will be so even though part of the communicative failure is due to misperception of younger interlocutors as indifferent or hostile. The parsimonious person will see the failure as due to an attitude on the other's part, not to anything on their own part aside from being of a certain age. The parsimonious individual will then be reinforced in perception of the young as indifferent or hostile. And accompanying negative attitudes toward the young will be strengthened by the bitterness and frustration of the experience. There will also be ancillary effects. The parsimonious individual will begin to question his or her self-worth when repeatedly rebuffed or misunderstood. He or she will come to accept the blame for communicative failure, but in a distorted manner. The blame will not be related to unfortunate practices but rather will be related to what the individual takes himself or herself to *be*, namely, too old to be of interest to anyone beyond a few cronies or a spouse. Communicative failure forces the individual to consider herself or himself as *properly* an object of negative attitudes and thereby to accept a certain self-image.

But communication is blocked in ways not resolvable by exercising greater care, being clearer, and the like. Parsimony is like blindness. The totally blind do not live in perpetual darkness; the visual dimension is simply missing. In like manner parsimony precludes comprehension by excluding recognition of meaningfulness. As Karl Mannheim says in another connection, some things are "accessible only to certain historic-social structures of consciousness."[5] The parsimoniously structured consciousness insures that much is inaccessible.

To understand better the way that parsimony is a kind of blindness, it is necessary to distinguish between factors contributing to communicative failure that are influences on the parsimonious individual and factors that are of his or her own making. With regard to the first, it is clearly difficult for a man or woman of seventy or eighty to be properly listened to in our present culture. This is exactly because of the presuppositions regarding the elderly or parsimonious that I am concerned to question. These presuppositions establish limits within which discourse between the young and the old takes place and are best thought of as external factors. Internal factors are the self-perception of the old as well as the character and plot assignations made in dealing with others. The external and internal overlap in that many older people *themselves* believe what younger people believe about advanced age. That is, they accept the culturally determined plots and characters that underlie the expectations of the young. This is in part because those plots and characters were integral to their intellectual development as children and young adults, both in terms of education and in the shaping of self-perception. I referred to the latter phenomenon in the previous chapter in speaking of the Foster Grandparents Plan's social workers coming to view themselves as they earlier did the volunteer grandparents. But the acceptance of stereotypes of the aged is also dependent on outside cues. As John McLeish puts it, "the self-image of the old is largely derived from the thousands of messages they see and hear in the eyes and actions and from the lips of the young."[6]

The external imposition of stereotypes or ready-made plots and characters makes parsimony more restrictive than it might be purely on the basis of successful coping. An individual's personal history determines plot employment, but his or her culture largely determines the kinds of plots that may be employed. A person's place in society and her or his educational background supply numerous plots, enhance the possibility of the employment or creation of others, and inhibit or preclude still others. There is indirect recognition of this in our society in various ways. For instance, certain sorts of decisions are deemed best made by individuals whose experience and position are of a certain sort. We doubt the ability of people with limited educational backgrounds to understand fully certain issues and questions. Judgements about competence are always complemented by judgements about "experience". The latter are judgements about an individual's wherewithal to deal with situations. Assessment of an actor or actress nicely shows what is under consideration. If a given individual is being considered for a part in, say, a Shakespearean play, it will be asked if he or she has done serious roles. Regardless of what we might think of her or his talent, someone who has done only television comedy would strike us as not a good bet to play Lady MacBeth or Hamlet. Here we have explicit assessment of future performance in terms of past plots and roles. We should see that assessing individuals in nonacting situations is also done in terms of previous plots and roles. As we judge that a television comedy star probably lacks the experience to do serious drama, we judge that a man or woman who has always worked in a subordinate capacity will be unable to make effective managerial decisions. He or she will not have played supervisory roles nor dealt with people cast as underlings. Personal plot history and external plot and character imposition insure that a man or woman of seventy-five, who has lived in a culture that casts the old as inherently weakened and vaguely incompetent, will see himself or herself in just that way.

Our culture does not provide the old with diverse and rich enough roles. Even ways of being exceptional are restricted with respect to the elderly. This is perhaps most easily seen in the preclusion of creativity in the old. To quote McLeish again,

The most tragic paradox of modern Western society is the contrast between the creative potentiality of older adults and the immobilizing effect upon them of social attitudes which stigmatize the later years as years of decline and fall, of accumulating decay, desuetude, and defeat.[7]

An older person is allowed to be exceptional but in a circumscribed way, namely, as eccentric. Otherwise the exceptional old person is seen as simply having retained one or another youthful attribute. A seventy-five-year-old is given the benefit of the doubt about mental abilities as a seventy-five-year-old if he or she behaves in ways sufficiently different from the norm to force the concession. Unfortunately, this is a role open largely to the rich and powerful. The poor have little opportunity to establish themselves as eccentric in the requisite ways because their activities tend to be invariably mundane and so limit the possibilities of significant departures from the norm. Eccentricity in a rich man or woman is senility in a poor one.

Communicative failure, then, is a function of both plot use and acceptance of imposed plots and characters that determine self-image as well as how others are perceived and addressed. Both the internal and external factors render us blind to important dimensions of others and of ourselves. We address and hear ourselves and others in ways that preclude productive interaction. Our interaction is between caricatures of persons, not persons.

Parsimony as a kind of blindness resulting in communicative failure is basically a matter of a break in the hermeneutical circle. The parsimonious individual cannot provide adequate anticipation of meaning to facilitate understanding, because he or she is blind to too much of what is meaningful for others and because his or her self-image is equally distorted. Without adequate anticipation the parsimonious individual cannot properly understand his or her interlocutors or even recognize who or what they are.[8] The consequence is that the parsimonious individual cannot address others effectively; he or she always addresses characters in his or her own plots. Nor can the individual understand herself or himself; he or she is confined to unproductive roles and thinks and speaks as a narrowed character. Before parsimony becomes counterproductive, available and generated characters coincide well enough with actual interlocutors and oneself for communication to be effective. But as the gap between characters and real people widens because of more and more paring and gerrymandering of plots and character types, it is less and less possible to reach others. And the failure to do so, as noted above, both supports the expectations of others that the parsimonious individual is incapable of effective communication and affects self-image. The incapacity is then attributed first to lack of interest, then to vagueness and inattention, and finally to senility.

The irony is that communicative failure is a result of successful plot use. And because it is success that underlies the parsimony, we effectively preclude consideration of the failure as due to restrictive and preemptive practices and images. Given that preclusion, we seem to have only one option: namely, to blame others and ourselves, but ourselves only with respect to what we think we are, not what we do.

The external influences or paucity of available roles for the old is cultural parsimony and as such is another aspect of parsimony. This external side of parsimony is, for the most part, well enough known. We often bemoan role playing, as if there were something that was *not* role playing. We confuse the desirability of flexibility in role playing with the imagined desirability and possibility of role-less interaction. We conceive roles very vaguely, borrowing heavily from half-understood theories in the social sciences. But roles do provide a scapegoat. We blame role playing for the inability to change the ways interaction proceeds, and we think we have both explained something and identified the only villain in doing so. We see only the external influence. If we give a thought to our own part, it is as victims, as subjects of impositions. We may acknowledge that we are, after all, active in playing a role, but we then blame peer pressure, the lack of alternatives, and so on. We resist acknowledging the utility of role playing with respect to coping, for that sounds too much like acknowledging "inauthenticity". We *want* to be victims, in order not to be accomplices. But of course this is yet another instance of coping by being parsimonious. We deal with the difficulty and protect ourselves at the same time by casting ourselves as characters manipulated by society, culture, history, or simply the needs and expectations of someone close to us.

Cultural parsimony raises questions well beyond the scope of my project. I have touched on the notion mainly because this sort of parsimony is familiar enough, and reference to it is useful in clarifying the notion of parsimony in the personal realm.

In the next chapter I shall attempt to deal with a number of problems and questions, central among them being the matter of the value of my proposal about narrative employment and its specific importance to a productive attitude toward perspective changes in aging.

6

The Value of Plot Talk

To conclude my project I must consider a number of matters, chief among them being how plot talk applies specifically to perspective change in aging and why it is advantageous to adopt my proposal about narrative employment. The latter must be made out because it may seem there is little practical difference between speaking of perspective change in terms of plot use and plot creation and using various presently available models and metaphors. I shall begin with the more practical of these two questions: namely, why my proposal is advantageous.

In considering the question of advantage, one must keep in mind that my proposal is a pragmatic one and that the point of its adoption is to put in place a vocabulary that will enable us to talk about perspective change in aging in ways that satisfy the conditions outlined in chapter 1. Those consisted of adequate interpretive latitude, recognition of aging as natural as opposed to pathological, and prevention of invidious isolation of the old. The standard to be met is productivity, as opposed to descriptive accuracy. I am not proffering my narrative account as a *true description* but as a construal of mental processes. The parallel is, as mentioned before, with Freud's psychological dynamics. The account is a construction to be put on thought and action, a construction designed to displace current ones because of its greater productivity. That some may take current constructions to be true descriptions does not preclude an alternative's being introduced in a pragmatic mood.

The first point I want to make is that plot talk is thoroughly anti-Cartesian. It shatters our imagined integrity as minds supposedly constituted of self-conscious thought. In this way plot talk helps us to avoid one entailment of the Cartesian picture, namely, conception of perspective changes as consequences of intentional cognitive activity. If we acknowledge the rather messy nature of consciousness, we can also acknowledge that some perspectives are structures that mold self-consciousness rather than being merely instances of self-consciousness. Conception of the mind as at least largely transparent to itself entails that the way we can handle perspectives that are operant in conditioning consciousness, and of which their subjects are unaware, is in terms of self-deception or suppression. Narrowing of perspective must then be construed as a cognitive *failing* of a mainly intentional sort. This view underlies exhortations to the old to "take an interest". These exhortations attribute the consequences of parsimony to increasing mental apathy or even laziness and suggest that what is needed to counter those consequences is only greater effort. There simply is no room in the Cartesian conception for plot use that regularly determines thought patterns without itself being intentional. In a word, no cognitive activity can contribute to the constitution of "the mind" without being either self-conscious or somehow suppressed. This may well be a thoroughly outmoded conception, but that does not prevent its being at work in the thinking of many.

Unlike the Cartesian conception, my narrative employment proposal not only tolerates but requires that some constitutive activities of "the mind" are not intentional. Basic plot use will not be so, as it is the matter of reflective thought. Moreover plot use *need* not be intentional at any given level.

But are our present ways of speaking about perspective change inherently Cartesian? My difficulty is that it is quite impossible to demonstrate that they are, for commonly used expressions need not entail Cartesian presuppositions in themselves, and it is as impossible to "prove intent" with respect to their use, to borrow a phrase from the language of the courts. My claim must be that there is sufficient reason to be suspicious of our current vocabulary and its attitudinal implications with respect to perspective change in aging, and therefore there is sufficient reason to propose an alternative vocabulary that will facilitate the improvement of attitudes. The parallel is to feminists seeking to change ways of speaking to root out sexist presuppositions. As for the sufficiency of reason for proposing a new vocabulary, certainly something is amiss in how we now deal with the aged, given the efforts expended in identifying and trying to change prejudicial attitudes and practices regarding them. There are too many works to cite devoted to considering how one or another aspect of our culture casts the aged in unfortunate roles (but see note 1 of chapter 3). To give just one example, Robin Henig's *The Myth of Senility*, subtitled *Misconceptions About the Brain and Aging*, tries to dispel the myth that growing old just is growing senile, a project that is very like my own attempt to detach interpretive parsimony from aging as such.[1] Something *is* amiss in how we think of and treat those among us who are of advanced age. Nonetheless, the obvious objection to my proposal is that present attitudes are not as prejudicial and inhibitive of understanding aging as I make out. And this objection cannot be met with inventories of expressions or, for that matter, inventories of cases in point, though enough of the latter might suffice. I have to tell a new story; I have to develop a narrative that encompasses our present attitudes and renders them intelligible in a new way, in the process of enabling us to deal with perspective change more productively. The only way to meet the objection is to tell a story that establishes the need for its own telling by its productivity.

I must now concede that our present views on perspective change are rather closer to what I have proposed than I have so far suggested. We do currently think in terms of interpretive practices growing to counterproductive levels through successful coping, even though we may not call the process interpretive parsimony or understand it in terms of plot use and creation. We do describe people as coming to have narrower perspectives because of the ways they deal with experience. In particular, we tie growing perspective narrowness to occupations. We expect that someone who has worked at one or another job for two or three decades will have narrower perspectives in certain areas because of limitations, priorities, and requirements for success imposed by the job in question. We also think, as was noted above, that people are hampered in their ability to deal with some sorts of situations by their familiarity and success with other sorts of situations. Interpretive parsimony could be made out to be quite familiar and even attributed to success in coping with experience, so my proposal might look like merely the explicit articulation of what is implicit in our current thinking.

However, our current thinking with respect to perspective change is two-tiered. Even though we may think of such change as due to experience in a certain range of cases, we crucially do not do so in another range. We begin to use a different model when we deal with people in their late sixties and older. We seem to think that experience is responsible for perspective change up to a point, but that beyond that point a new factor enters the picture. It is not clear precisely what this new factor is taken to be, but it is thought of as more directly causal in nature than the accumulation of experience. The factor is essentially *debility*. It may not be more sharply conceived than as a vague deterioration. The general inclination is to see the wear on our bodies as having degenerative consequences on our minds. Even the most dualistic, as in the case of the staunchly religious, see bodily deterioration as impairing mental activity. There is a very powerful tendency to equate physical deterioration with mental debility in spite of opposing cognitive or emotional commitments to a mind or soul substantially distinct from the body. The underlying assumption is Platonic, namely, that the mind, regardless of how distinct from the body, is impaired by the body at the best of times. The materialist, of course, needs no special account of how physical deterioration relates to mental deterioration. However, what matters is that neither dualists nor monists feel a need to justify equating or closely linking physical and mental deterioration. And this is not *just* a mistake. We are undeniably physical beings, and whatever our ontology, age results in some physical deterioration and must therefore result in some mental deterioration. Not even the most sanguine would deny that advanced age results in changes that constitute significant impairment. The perception of physical debility properly raises the question of mental debility. I am certainly not quixotically arguing against the obvious. What I am arguing for is greater perspicacity. We altogether too quickly introduce debility as an explanatory factor on the basis of mere chronological age.

Our present view of the aged could be well grounded at least in how those of advanced years have participated in our form of life in the past. But that participation has changed, whether in our perception of it or in fact. The present generation of people in their late sixties and beyond are healthier, more active, and also more conscious of themselves as objects of prejudice than previous generations of the elderly. This may be due to no more than the fact that this generation constitutes a larger proportion of the population than before and is therefore receiving greater and better attention. But what is undeniable is that proportionate changes are called for in how we construe what these people say and do.

I might sum up by saying that our present view of perspective change is both inadequate and simplistic. The simplistic aspect has to do with indiscriminate attribution of perspective change in later life to ill-defined debility; the inadequate aspect has to do with the failure to extend the understanding of perspective change in early and middle life to later life. Our present view of perspective change can be seen as inadequate and simplistic through the introduction of an explanatory device that enables us to extend the use of experience to understand perspective changes in later life as we do in early and middle life. We can then avoid the facile use of debility with respect to changes in later life. The impetus for telling the new story is the conviction that something is amiss with our attitudes toward the old because of our current two-tiered way of construing perspective change. In my story our present picture of perspective change in aging is a hastily generalized one based on chronological age and dubious assumptions about its consequences. The picture amounts to the belief that those consequences explain everything in the behaviour of people whose age is manifestly advanced and who act at odds with our expectations. In other words, failure to meet those expectations is attributed to debility seen as entailed by chronological age. In my story this attitude is shown to be inadequate by the introduction of a newly articulated explanatory factor, namely, interpretive parsimony grown counterproductive. This new factor demands prior application in explaining what fails to meet expectations. That is, it is introduced as a simpler and likelier cause of what is usually attributed to the consequences of sheer aging. The new explanatory factor requires that what does not meet our expectations first be considered as amenable to interpretation, as opposed to being seen as simply pathological in some vague sense. Only if such interpretation is unproductive or impossible are we justified in attributing the behaviour in question to debility of some sort. And even then what sort of debility is involved must be made out fairly carefully.

The preceding remarks about stories relate directly to a thesis expounded by Alasdair MacIntyre. MacIntyre considers what he calls epistemological crises to be resolvable by the use of narratives. An epistemological crisis is a time when "the relationship of *seems* to *is* becomes crucial."[2] It is a time when a given set of events admit of various rival interpretations and the differences among the rivals are of major significance. MacIntyre begins to develop his notion by asking us to consider what it is to share a culture and goes on to say that it is "to share schemata which are at one and the same time constitutive of and normative for intelligible action."[3] Given such schemata, epistemological crises arise when someone comes to recognize "the possibility of systematically different possibilities of interpretation, of the existence of alternative . . . schemata which yield mutually incompatible accounts of what is going on."[4] He uses Hamlet's return from Wittenberg as a case in point and argues that until Hamlet "has adopted some schema he does not know what to treat as evidence; [but] until he knows what to treat as evidence he cannot tell which schema to adopt."[5] It is in this crisis situation that MacIntyre sees the role of narrative as decisive, for the crucial question is "How ought the narrative of these events to be constructed?"[6] His contention is that when an epistemological crisis is resolved, it is by the construction of a new narrative which enables the agent to understand *both* how he or she could intelligibly have held his or her original beliefs *and* how he or she could have been so drastically misled by them. The narrative in terms of which he or she at first understood and ordered experience is itself made into the subject of an enlarged narrative.[7]

I am proposing a schema that objectifies our present understanding of perspective change in aging and enables us to understand prejudicial attitudes toward the elderly. These attitudes are seen as consequences of attribution of unexpected behaviour to debility rather than to success in coping with experience.[8] When the use of debility as a general explanatory device becomes the object of reflection consequent on the introduction of parsimony as a rival device, we see that the reliance on debility constitutes only one possible schema. The introduction of plot talk constitutes a possible rival schema by allowing us to attribute unexpected behaviour, first, to the consequences of successful coping patterns and, only second and selectively, to more carefully characterized debility. The proposal underscores the fact that now that medicine, technology, and better nutrition have made our later years considerably more viable, the participation in culture of many people in their seventies, eighties, and even nineties demands a new interpretation, a new schema. We can no longer dismiss the old as incompetent and ineffectual because of age and then treat competent old people as exceptional. The present schema is failing us because the exceptions it tolerates outnumber the standard cases it describes. We need a new schema in which the aged are just older people, rather than members of a special class characterized by debility.

It might be argued that nothing has really changed, that it is only our perception of the aged that has altered because of cultural factors, such as greater concern with human rights or simply a greater number of old people. But this is beside the point, for what is crucial is precisely the change in perception of the aged. The trouble is that the change is incomplete; we are in a transition phase (on the most optimistic reading). Like

Hamlet, we have not adopted a schema but only begun to find the entrenched one inadequate. My proposal is intended to help force the completion of the transition to a new one.

It is open to anyone to propose a new schema, on recognition of need or only as a creative proposal made in the hope of improvement where none is readily envisaged. But the test for any such schema is consequential. The proposal must be productive. It must have greater scope and power than its entrenched competitor. The new schema must enable us to understand both the power and the inadequacy of the old one. I believe my proposal meets these criteria in enabling us to understand the inadequacy of the old schema by revealing how experience is too readily abandoned as an explanatory principle and debility uncritically adopted in its place. The proposal also enables us to understand the power of the old narrative by highlighting the rigidity imposed by counterproductive parsimony.

The claimed advantage of my proposed schema brings up in a pressing way the question of pragmatism. One objection will be that talk of advantage is a claim that the new schema is *for the better*, and many will feel that this implication is incompatible with pragmatism. Furthermore, some will feel that underlying much of the preceding is an implicit recognition that what is forcing the telling of a new story is a new *objective* reality that we come to discern and that in effect the claims about the advantages of the new story amount to the claim that it more accurately describes that reality. These points are an imposition of the limitations of the correspondence theory of truth on my proposal, by construal of what prompts the telling of a new story as a new objective state of affairs that is then viewed as more faithfully portrayed in the new story. In this way a construal of language as essentially representational is also imposed. And there is the added charge of nihilism in the preclusion that a pragmatist can judge one story better than another in any meaningful way.

The issues raised here are huge, and I cannot hope to settle them. At best I can clarify my pragmatic claims. To begin with, pragmatism, at least in its new incarnation, is a metaphilosophical position. The pragmatist is not concerned with introducing into the doing of what we can call "normal" philosophy, on the model of Thomas Kuhn's notion of "normal science", considerations that would cripple such philosophizing.[9] The pragmatist is mainly concerned with serving as a latter-day Socrates bent on keeping us from taking certain activities too seriously and thinking their products ultimate in an impossible way. But the pragmatist's is a very high level role or mission. A practicing physicist needs to see his or her work as limning the structure of reality, just as a moral philosopher needs to see his or her efforts as leading to the discernment of absolute principles. Otherwise the danger is that practitioners will turn nihilistic and think that in the end there is nothing to choose between one set of beliefs or values and another. This is of course not so; there is a great deal to choose. But the bases for choices and justifications are our values and beliefs, not ahistorical, ultimate principles accessible only to the purest reasoning. The heady thought the pragmatist supplies is that those values and beliefs are always open to reappraisal and revision. We must never think that we have finally hit on principles or truths that are inviolate and absolute. Happily enough, we cannot long hold the pragmatic view, and invariably we return to doing "normal" science or philosophy. But the pragmatist serves a necessary role: The pragmatist is at hand to prevent our tying ourselves up in knots. He or she is Nietzsche, the later Wittgenstein, or Rorty, employing shock tactics to remind us that our understanding, values, and justificatory procedures are historical. They also remind us of our complete immersion in language, our inability to get out of language and compare its constructions to a neutral world.

The pragmatist judges our activities on the standard of productivity, but that is not the one transcendent principle available. It is simply the measure of our success given particular aims and values. This mundane point is the only counter to the charge of nihilism or the claim that pragmatism precludes judging one story better than another because pragmatism rejects ultimate standards. The point is simply that we have the values we have and that we have the justificatory procedures we have. The openness to revision of these values and procedures does not vitiate them as grounds and methods of judgement. What lends spurious force to the view that openness to revision does vitiate them is the insistence by the nonpragmatist on raising questions about value and justification in the abstract, allowing the questions no content and accepting only wholly general principles as answers. *Of course* we can judge one story better than another. We do so, for instance, on the basis of whether one enables us to respect the dignity of older people better than its rival. That the dignity we value may itself sometime be an object of reappraisal does not mean that it does not serve as a basis for judgement while in place. The nonpragmatist conjures up visions of a hopeless relativism and an imagined preparedness to abandon values for arbitrary reasons. But this is a perverse view. The nonpragmatist's own efforts illustrate the grip our values have and our resistance to altering or abandoning them. Moreover, values are hierarchical, and they are not all at issue at one time. Questions about dignity may arise if we find—for instance, in war or under catastrophic conditions—that we must compromise or reassess what we think human beings are due. But that questions may arise does not mean that dignity cannot serve as a basis for judgement when it is not itself under scrutiny.

There is a kind of petulance in the charge of nihilism. The charge amounts to saying that if we cannot be given absolute guarantees that what we prize is ultimately and forever desirable, we must spitefully cease to prize it. It is as if the moment divorce was conceived, marriage ceased to be an expression of love and commitment.

The preceding should suggest that there is an important difference to note between the pragmatism of my proposal and pragmatism as a metaphilosophical perspective. My proposal is more circumscribed and has a practical objective. But it relies on metaphilosophical pragmatism to keep at bay critics demanding experimental evidence of the correctness of my suggestions—on the assumption that my proposal is a *descriptive* one. In describing my proposal as the proffering of a new pragmatic vocabulary, I mean that the vocabulary is not intended as a new and more accurate description of something determinate but poorly described by our present vocabulary. I mean that given the elusiveness and indeterminacy of the subject of discourse, my vocabulary is more fruitful as a way of thinking and speaking, and it avoids a number of difficulties. To refer to Freud again, I am offering a dynamic model or construction to be employed, but it is one to be tested on the basis of how it works, as Freud's psychological dynamic construction was tested on the basis of its clinical results. Freud did think that eventually the structure of the mind would be traced neurophysiologically, but he did *not* think that there were exact neurophysiological correlates of the elements in his psychological model. The dynamics of id, ego, and superego exhaust the psychoanalytic model. We cannot look in the brain for the counterparts of the id, ego, and superego and expect to find something that both is physical and constitutes the id as such, or the superego as such. In like manner, I am not suggesting that there are neutrally discernible processes that are the employment of narratives and that may be confirmed experimentally. The narrative employment vocabulary is proffered as a useful dynamic model, not as a better descriptive theory the offering of which follows on the collating of new data. Basically this is all that can be said against the imposition of correspondence-theory requirements and the representational conception of language on my proposal.

The above remarks may suffice with respect to my proposal to the extent that even a confirmed correspondence theorist will allow that some models or vocabularies may be useful even if not descriptive; witness the Freudian scheme and numerous heuristic models used in physics. As a pragmatist, I could be content with that sufficiency. However, I need at least to endorse metaphilosophical pragmatism.

The nub of the issue between myself and the nonpragmatist is that talk of advantage or productivity is heard by the latter as entailing accuracy of representation as well as objective values that constitute the backdrop of the evaluation. Any advantage claimed for my account is seen as advantage in virtue of the accuracy of the account, and advantage claimed is taken to commit the claimer to objective values or to force the admission of relativism. The nonpragmatist, then, expects that in proffering my narrative employment vocabulary, I must make clear the value-background assumed, as well as support the proposed vocabulary with data that indicates some conformity of that vocabulary to "reality". Evidence of a need for that vocabulary is also expected. It is precluded that the proposal can flow from general dissatisfaction and that it need only be successful to be justified.

The wider issue is that the nonpragmatist disallows value claims by the pragmatist as inconsistent with the contention that values are not grounded on anything more than practice. Supposedly this contention renders all values mere preferences to be understood as individually subjective or relative to some group. The trouble with the latter ("cultural relativism") is that the nonpragmatist considers it always proper to ask of some group's values whether those values are correct. In other words, the unviability of relativism is the alleged possibility that a given group may value something and be *wrong*. This is, of course, to presuppose objectivism and preclude any alternative. The underlying view is that value cannot be relative to history and culture without being "arbitrary". This is a typical philosophical distortion of a complex reality by the imposition of principles themselves imagined to be free of history and culture. But as Rorty says,

there is ... no criterion that we have not created in the course of creating a practice, no standard of rationality that is not an appeal to such a criterion, no rigorous argumentation that is not obedience to our own conventions.[10]

Our problem is that we project our standards and practices outward; we see them reflected in the world and conclude that since they cannot be in the world as so much furniture, they must be beyond the world as features of a greater reality.

But the pragmatist is not restricted to *mere* preferences, whether individual or collective. He or she has all the value we find in culture and history. And that value has all the power and permanence we give it in holding it as we do. What the pragmatist eschews is the idea that anything in culture or history is grounded on something outside of culture and history, on some transcendency, whether it be a god or Platonic forms or pure reason. It is *we* who decide what is of value and what constitutes proper procedures, and that does not mean that we are at the mercy of whim. To see the pragmatic position as hopelessly nihilistic because it forgoes ahistorical, extracultural, atemporal foundations for values and attendant justificatory procedures is to exhibit a peculiarly religious penchance, namely, the tendency to view anything human as insufficient and to believe that anything of real worth must be superhuman. What underlies this penchance is a profound distrust of our own worth and particularly of our constancy.

As admitted above, the larger issues will not be resolved here. It must be enough that my proposal is taken as pragmatic in the narrower sense and on the model of a heuristic device and that the value that prompts it is that human beings should not be the objects of prejudice, whether on the basis of race, creed, or chronological age. I must now turn to a pressing but more manageable question: namely, how my narrative proposal applies specifically to aging.

The question of the application of my proposal to aging and the changes it brings has two parts. The first is about the point of the proposal and the kind of difference its adoption should make; the second has to do with the particular implementation of plot talk. The first part admits of rather brief treatment, given what has been said so far.

The broadest way to describe the application of the proposal is that in interacting with people significantly older than ourselves, we should first interpret their remarks and behaviour in terms of parsimonious practices and not in terms of debility. The effect of this perspective shift is perhaps best illustrated by cases where acquiring background information alters our attitude toward an individual. For instance, we may find a given person's aloofness offensive until we learn that he or she has great difficulty overcoming shyness. We then understand the aloofness to be prompted by something other than arrogance or unfriendliness. In fact, we cease to see the person as aloof; instead we see him or her as inhibited. Our attitude changes, and so does our behaviour. We try to make it easier for the person to relate to us; we show friendliness more openly. In the same way, when we understand that an elderly person's difficult ways may be due to parsimony, we work harder at relating to and understanding the person in question. But in both cases the change has a depth not captured by describing it in terms of greater sympathy and empathy. Our perception of the person changes. The person becomes someone with whom we seek to interact, rather than being someone with whom we must deal.

The complication in the case of the aged is that application of my proposal cannot be only a matter of recognizing parsimony. Not all communicative problems with people of advanced age are due to parsimony. Advanced age does bring debility to many. Just as the assumption of debility masks the role of parsimony, the assumption of parsimony could mask debility. My proposal has a change of perception as its point, but, as noted in chapter 1, it should not blind us to real problems.

In dealing with an old man or woman who appears "confused", we must work at understanding to what extent parsimony is an appropriate explanatory device and to what extent other factors are operant.[11] Parsimony and debility are mutually reinforcing. Parsimonious practices may be made more rigid by debility, and those practices may broaden the consequences of debility by reducing the efficacy of an individual's efforts to compensate for debility. It will clearly be most difficult to gauge the extent of debility and the extent of parsimony; therefore our procedure must be to think in terms of parsimony as a matter of course. This point brings out the interpretive and impositional character of my proposal. Adoption of the proposal is a *decision* to see and treat the aged in a certain manner. It is to superimpose on perception of advanced age an overriding construal of the aged as parsimonious first and only secondly debilitated. This interpretive superimposition will alter our perception so that age will cease to be an objectifying characteristic and come to be an occasion for more deliberate interpretation. This readiness for a kind of communicative generosity will, of course, have *some* unfortunate objectifying effects, but these should be no worse than those involved in dealing with persons who do not share our language or some aspect of our culture.

The adoption of my proposal should result in a change of

perception, and this change will entail changes in practice. Coming to see the aged as possibly hampered by narrow and rigid patterns of thought and behaviour and not necessarily by dimmed senses and muddled thinking makes it possible to deal with them as persons with problems rather than as problems themselves. However, while an understanding of interpretive parsimony has been depicted as central to the perspective change, I have not made clear how plot talk applies to aging other than as a way of construing the nature of parsimony. I must now say something about the practical side of plot talk with respect to aging.

We all know of how elderly people become more alert and communicative when involved in some project or when interacting with people to whom they relate easily. There is marked improvement in mood and behaviour when an isolated old person finds herself or himself in a stimulating environment. To refer again to the Foster Grandparents Program, it unquestionably does as much for the volunteer grandparents as for the children it helps. Where the alternative for a man or woman of seventy may be lonely idleness, working with young children in need of help and guidance can be an extremely productive activity. But the improvement in someone who becomes involved in an activity of the sort in question cannot be attributed to a sudden lessening of debility. To think this is to continue to identify aging with increasing debility. There is the case, for instance, where installation of video games in a home for the aged resulted in noticeable improvements in hand/eye coordination and related capacities among the residents.[12] What such cases show is that an elderly man or woman who interacts only with other elderly persons as parsimonious as himself or herself and whose basic needs are seen to by attendants has little or no occasion to deal with the world in productive ways. Even a video game is significant stimulation to such an individual. The video game does not reverse any physiological deterioration present; it prompts efforts of a sort not called for prior to the game's introduction. And those efforts lead to improved performance, as exercise improves a muscle. Introduction of a new stimulus raises functional levels closer to what they were before restricted stimulation reduced them and allowed any debility present to dominate the individual's attitude and behaviour.

Unquestionably aging to some extent dims our vision, muffles our hearing, and slows our thinking and acting. Perhaps most importantly, aging seems to impair our short-term memory and our ability to assimilate easily events that seem to occur ever more quickly. But we can either accelerate the process by acquiescing or try to deal with that impairment. Once it is recognized that some of that impairment is due to our own practices, to parsimony, meaningful efforts can be made to cope with such things as decreased memory and sensory efficiency. We *are* able to cope with some of the unfortunate effects of living long enough to have survival itself become a source of difficulty. But to do so we must see that aging does not entail wholesale mental and physical deterioration. We must sort out problems that can be dealt with from those that must be borne. And this is where research is crucial in enabling us to discriminate. But prior to that discrimination, the use of the pragmatic notion of interpretive parsimony can dispel the idea that just growing old makes us rigid and narrow in our thinking and can show us how we might become rigid and narrow, thereby enabling us to work at reversing parsimony. Problems such as benign memory loss, and perhaps even the milder forms of malignant memory loss, may be coped with if perceived as circumscribed difficulties and not as aspects of a holistic and inevitable "senility".

Unlike debility, parsimony is reversible to the extent that stimulation raises functional levels. Parsimony is the narrowing of thought and behaviour patterns, so any broadening of such patterns will be a reversal of parsimony. But for significant reversal, the overly parsimonious person must recognize that he or she has grown parsimonious. He or she must think of our dealing with experience by implementing narratives and must realize that success may lead to the implementation of fewer and eventually too few narratives. That way of thinking will have two crucial effects. First, it will enable the person in question to attribute the consequences of parsimony to something other than irreversible debility; second, it will enable the person to counteract parsimony in a deliberate manner. The introduction of the notion of parsimony, as well as training in remedial practices, could be undertaken in what I will call "narrative therapy". Such therapy might consist of group training in deliberate envisagement of alternative plots. The objective would be to reestablish breadth of interpretive latitude.

In sensitivity training, one technique is to pair off participants and have them initiate conversation, then to introduce a third party into each conversation, and next to take one of the parties away from each group. Later there is general discussion of whether newcomers were felt to be intruding, how departure of group members was perceived, and so on. The objective is to enhance sensitivity to the dynamics of change in groups and to prompt better understanding of the perception and consequences of events such as births and deaths in a family context or hirings and firings in a workplace.[13] Similar techniques could be used with parsimonious individuals to initiate awareness of narrative employment. Participants might have a situation related or depicted and then be asked to tell stories about the situation. The resulting exposure to a variety of interpretations will heighten participants' awareness of their own construals of situations. The point throughout would be to get individuals who have grown parsimonious to understand that they *are* imposing plots, that they *are* implementing narratives, assigning roles, and so on. Once this realization is achieved, discussion of possible alternatives to particular stories can bring out how plot use may grow restricted and need to be broadened. Once a participant appreciates that his or her story is one of a number of possible ones, he or she can better appreciate how the telling of a particular story indicates interpretive inclinations and how these may be restrictive.

The actual mechanics of the therapy might go something like this: Given a depicted situation, say, presented as a photographic slide (as in the case referred to in chapter 3), participants would recount their interpretations of the situation. That recounting would be narrational, in that—even putting aside my proposal—the only way we have of making sense to others of a situation so presented is to produce a narrative that encompasses and orders what is presented. MacIntyre puts the point as follows:

in successfully identifying and understanding what someone else is doing we always move towards placing a particular episode in the context of a set of narrative histories. . . . [W]e render the actions of others intelligible in this way because action itself has a basically historical character. It is because we all live out narratives in our lives and because we understand our own lives in terms of the narratives that we live out that the form of narrative is appropriate for understanding the actions of others.[14]

Once participants have articulated their narratives, the discussion leader or therapist has three consecutive objectives. The first is to prompt or heighten awareness of the diversity of the stories told, even if this means exaggerating minor differences. The second objective is to prompt reflection on the narrative nature of the interpretations recounted. And the third objective is to prompt consideration of possible alternatives to the stories told by individual participants. Given parsimony, the third objective will be the most difficult to achieve, but its achievement will be facilitated by the achievement of the first objective. Once these objectives have been achieved in open discussion, the leader or therapist will be in a position to pursue, perhaps privately with each participant, the various factors involved in determining the form of each story told and some of the alternatives. The result of the exercise should be growing awareness on the part of the individual of how narratives are employed to order experience and how that employment is heavily influenced by prior success in dealing with experience.

In an ideal world corrective therapy would not be needed; we would grow up using vocabularies that would always remind us of the various interpretive structures we impose. In a less than ideal world, we can hope only to reverse parsimony to some extent in the case of the aged and to influence education to some degree with respect to inculcating productive expectations and patterns of thought in the young. These should inhibit the tendency to carry parsimony to counterproductive extremes and more particularly should preempt prejudicial ideas of what it is to grow and be old.

The use of narrative in various forms of therapy is widespread, but what distinguishes the narrative therapy just sketched is the underlying construal of narrative employment as basic to conceptualization and the organization of experience. If it is thought that we employ narrative only as one mode of presentation among others, then parsimony will not be recognized for what it is. At present sensitivity training and other forms of "consciousness raising", as well as diverse therapies, employ narrative in specific and directed ways. And some of these are precisely designed to heighten awareness of prejudicial or stereotypic thinking. But the use of narrative is invariably a tool to further the objectives of the therapy or training. Narrative is seen as a device that will make a point or highlight something. If the objective is to reduce stereotypic thinking, narrative may be used to indicate the consequences of such thinking or to illustrate such thinking. But my concern is with how a certain use of narrative is *itself* stereotypic thinking. My proposal and the notion of interpretive parsimony require that narrative employment be recognized as fundamental to dealing with experience. In other words, it must be seen as a device not only useful in dealing with certain problems, but so fundamental that it itself produces problems when its employment becomes counterproductive. The point of narrative therapy as I have sketched it is recognition of narrative employment as an experience-ordering activity. Only given such recognition can that activity be extended beyond limits imposed by its own success.

As noted, plot talk is necessary to characterize and understand the notion of interpretive parsimony. But its special application in dealing with perspective change in aging is more therapeutic than explanatory. Plot talk must become reflexive in the sense that there has to be self-conscious use of plot talk as we create and use plots. Plot talk must itself be used to increase awareness of plot use and creation. Individuals must be trained to distance themselves from their own construals of experience. Reflexive awareness that experience is structured is a prerequisite to deliberately influencing that structuring.

The particular application of plot talk to the problems of aging is basically its introduction at a reflective level through devices such as the therapy outlined above. The introduction of plot talk facilitates thinking of the structuring of experience narrationally. And given that way of thinking, plot talk facilitates some control over that structuring. If used in deliberate, ongoing self-description, for example, plot talk can define what we are up to and bring out discrepancies between what we are up to and what we only think we are up to. Rationalizations of prejudicial behaviour, for instance, are more difficult to maintain when articulated, even if only to ourselves.

But plot talk does not relate only to how we structure experience. It also enables us to understand better how we structure *ourselves* in that it unpacks self-image into diverse character roles.

To refer again to MacIntyre, his remarks about narrational self-definition, or what he calls the "narrative concept of selfhood", are indicative of how plot talk may facilitate insight into how each of us defines himself or herself. As acknowledged in note 8 to this chapter, MacIntyre's narrative thesis is very like my own. He tells us that "man is in his actions and practice, as well as in his fictions, essentially a story-telling animal" and warns: "Deprive children of stories and you leave them unscripted."[15] There is even a nod to pragmatism in that he adds that man "is not essentially, but becomes through his history, a teller of stories that aspire to truth."[16] But what interests me here is his concern with understanding the unity of an individual's life in terms of narrative. Though he is, in the context in question, primarily concerned with accountability, his narrative concept of selfhood turns on recognizing the self as having a unity which is

the unity of a character.... Just as a history is not a sequence of actions, but the concept of an action is that of a moment in an actual or possible history abstracted for some purpose from that history, so the characters in a history are not a collection of persons, but the concept of a person is that of a character abstracted from a history.[17]

The Cartesian idea that we are individual egos and that we can at any moment be *just* that, divorced from any story, is bizarre and could have been articulated only within a rarefied philosophical context. Outside of such a context, a Cartesian ego would be pathological. Each of us is, at any moment, what we remember ourselves to be. And that is to say we are the person defined by the memories operant at the time; this is in turn to say that we are the character determined by a particular story.[18] Just as the concept of *another* person is that of a character abstracted from a history, when we consider ourselves reflexively, *we* are characters abstracted from a narrative. And we must learn to recognize ourselves as characters. Doing so is crucial in two ways. First, as MacIntyre considers, each of us is not only the subject of a history but also a character in the narratives of others. Histories overlap one another; we play parts in the narratives of others, but of course not as subjects. Moreover, we are characters not so much abstracted from but constituted by perceived or imagined histories that we might not recognize as our own. We need to appreciate the variety of parts we play in others' narratives. Second, each of us is really several persons; each has a history that is internally diverse in attitudinal if not spatiotemporal ways. This diversity adds to our worth as human beings and enriches our lives. Parsimony erodes this diversity, as it erodes communicative success and interpretive flexibility. The parsimonious individual, in restricting his or her own narratives, restricts the parts he or she can play in the narratives of others as parsimony constricts his or her range of response and homogenizes the faces he or she presents to others. But parsimony also homogenizes complex selves. Recognition that we are characters in others' narratives is a step toward recognizing that we are characters in our *own* narratives and that we may restrict our parts through narrowed self-perception and rigid expectations. For instance, a man or woman who unknowingly accepts our culture's stereotype of old age, whose self-perception is shaped by that stereotype, will conform to numerous restrictive practices and *be* old in the stereotyped way.

Plot talk affects self-definition in two ways once it is introduced. In enabling us to conceptualize ourselves as characters in the narratives of others, it lets us reflect on how others see us in the context of their own lives, as opposed to our always maintaining an egocentric perspective on how we figure in those lives. We then more readily adjust our behaviour toward other people; we anticipate how their perception of us may enhance or inhibit communicative possibilities. Plot talk also enables us to recognize that we are subjects only within narratives, that a self at any given moment is a subject in the context of a story that determines the world for that subject-self. We can then better understand how memory and context determine attitudes and action and how, as these vary, we play different parts in the narratives that make up our own individual histories. And given that recognition, we better understand how an overly parsimonious self-image may restrict character diversity and thereby impoverish us.

Plot talk facilitates certain ways of thinking. Plot talk recasts the complex whole of our thought and action in terms of parts we play; and in doing so, plot talk objectifies aspects of our experience and distances us from them enough to allow reflection on those aspects. That reflection makes it possible for us to understand how age may change us by restricting our stories and the parts we play in them. We can then work at telling new stories.

Any pragmatic proposal faces difficulties of a philosophical sort, but it has the tremendous advantage of possibly succeeding in spite of those difficulties not being resolved according to nonpragmatic expectations. That is, a pragmatic proposal may be taken up and, in being taken up, may prove productive and simply displace its competitors. The history of philosophy amply illustrates this sort of success in that novel philosophical proposals have often been successful in the way a new *genre* is successful. Competitors remain unrefuted, but cease to be challenging or perhaps even of interest. As for specifically pragmatic proposals, Rorty points out,

It is just not the case that one need adopt one's opponent's vocabulary or method or style in order to defeat him. . . . Nietzsche and James did not have epistemological arguments for pragmatism. Each . . . presented us with a new form of intellectual life, and asked us to compare its advantages with the old.[19]

In this chapter I have tried to say something about the advantages of my narrative proposal and its application to aging. Of course the judgment of those advantages must follow application of the proposal. The aim here is to show the proposal plausible and worthy of being taken up. At the theoretical level its advantages can only be suggested and intuitive appreciation invited. But enough has been said in this chapter. I must now address a rather different topic, namely, the matter of how my narrative proposal relates to the ultimate challenge of growing old: impending death. However useful a proposal might be with respect to understanding aging, or even in alleviating some of its difficulties, if it is silent on death, it will be incomplete.

7

The Grim Reality

This chapter might be titled "No one survives old age." It is about how plot talk relates to the inevitable reality of death. Given our biological makeup, most people in their eighties and nineties may expect to die soon. This is the case in spite of their being in good health. Actuarial tables show that very few of us survive much beyond our eighth or ninth decade. It may be that science will succeed in increasing our life span, but at the moment to be eighty or ninety is to face the prospect that most of one's life is past. And with all due respect to Lucretius, we fear dying.[1] Regardless of how we might come to terms with dying, death does not lose its *force*.

In advanced age the inevitability of death is recognized in a way that it cannot be recognized earlier, when death is very remote. The recognition of death as near and inescapable must shape our perspectives as decisively as parsimony, in spite of sublimation or resignation. As noted in chapter 1, the realization that we "can't go on" is very much at odds with our instinct *to* go on. The realization may be blunted by sentimentality or by religious beliefs, but it is undeniably an immensely important influence on us in old age. If application of my narrative proposal to aging is to be realistic and complete, something must be said about this factor that affects our stories and roles as much as anything discussed in the previous chapters.

I want to begin with a general point about narrative. A likely rejoinder to what I have been proposing about narrative employment will be that we should make every effort to lessen our dependency on narrative, that our aim should be to further modes of thought and articulation that are not narrational. In other words, even if the essentials of my proposal are granted, they may be seen as impediments to be overcome. This view is as old as Plato's distrust of drama and poetry.

The opposition is between the particularity of narrative and the generality of putative ahistorical articulation of truth. Any generality that narrative might claim must be of the sort Aristotle allowed drama in assigning to it a capacity to reflect the universal in the particular. That is, narrative can claim generality only in offering paradigmatic cases. Narrative can directly present only the historical, the particular. The general must be conveyed through metaphor and other symbolic devices. Narratives may be parables or allegories, but they cannot be universal assertions. Plato counsels avoidance of narrative, then, in favour of a mode of thought and discourse that he thought alone capable of limning ultimate reality by propositionally capturing ahistorical and wholly general truths. Contrary to this view, the pragmatist campaigns for historicity and particularity, for productive stories. Rorty's critique of analytic philosophy and MacIntyre's critique of philosophical ethics are just such attempts to reinstate narrative, to show how the quest for ultimate truth is misconceived.

When I contrasted Platonic rationality with narrative in chapter 2, I argued that narrative is inherently pragmatic. And it is so partly because of its particularity. If one is committed to perspectiveless articulation of truth, as are Plato and Kant, narrative must look a poor second, for it requires and imposes perspective. Any *use* made of narrative must be pragmatic, for narrative, properly conceived, lacks a dimension of correctness. It limns nothing; rather than portraying realities, it presents realities. Statements of alleged ultimate truth, on the other hand, are supposedly useful to anyone anywhere at any time in virtue of their ahistorical, universal, and perspectiveless nature. But when we consider death, we find that statements offered as general and ahistorical seem to be of little use to the individual. Religion understood this, for the key doctrines it offered were the incorruptibility of the human spirit and an afterlife. The doctrines, though certainly general, offered people *personal* survival. If one is not disposed to believe in an afterlife, statements of alleged ultimate truth offer very cold comfort. And in failing to offer comfort, they manifest a fundamental irrelevance, for with regard to death, what does not comfort is simply of no use. We *understand* death well enough. What we want is something that will help us to bear dying and will help without lulling or deceiving us.

The preceding is a pragmatic case in point, in that it reveals the lack of productivity of "capital T" Truth. But my objective here is neither to continue the argument for pragmatism nor, for that matter, to try and offer comfort. What I must do is say something about how my narrative proposal relates to the prospect of impending death.

It seems that what is of greatest comfort to people facing death is whatever promises some sort of continuity. Most religions of course offer continuity, but beyond that the majority of people must be content with real or imagined continuity through their children, whether it be starkly conceived in terms of genetic survival or in more generous terms. A few find the promise of continuity in some work: a book, a painting, a system developed, even a record set. More attenuated is the comfort many take in being remembered by their friends. But the reality of sought-for continuity for the individual is in imagined and projected narratives: in speculations of a place in history or stories wherein daughters or grandsons "take after" her or him.

The preceding suggests that impending death may cast us more as authors of our narratives than protagonists in them. Perhaps we recede from our narratives in beginning to see them as continuing without us. Many scatter their hopes and objectives among their characters, and while those characters remain present to them, they imagine themselves less and less present to those characters. Some distance themselves from life through the conceit of trying to manipulate it, by trying to determine the course of events after their death. It may not be too much to say that the native tendency to narrate, to produce stories, is enhanced in old age as compensation for impending death. In a way it is all we have left, our last opportunity to determine reality for ourselves and others.

The change is most evident when concern with what will happen after our deaths becomes obsessional. We have instances of people who devote great chunks of their last years to complicated wills, endowments, and whatever sort of posthumous plans their resources may make possible. Retiring board chairpersons attempt to insure that companies will follow their policies; parents try to plan their childrens' lives. On a more pathetic scale are efforts to reify ourselves and continue to figure in the lives of others through something of ours or even our homilies ("This is my favorite ring; it will be yours when I'm gone"; "Remember that I always said . . . ").[2] We insinuate ourselves into the lives of others throughout our early and middle years, but in old age we do so with a narrower purpose and trade more openly on sentiment. But our efforts to live on through others do not entail greater involvement with them. Rather we objectify others in trying to mold their attitudes and manipulate their lives.[3]

Psychological theorizing about aging and impending death is very diverse, but there does seem to be some consensus on the increase of introversion in old age.[4] One way this introversion shows itself is in the tendency to review one's life.[5] And of course we must remember that in discussing such psychological factors, we are dealing with more than simple chronological age. A crucial question is the distance from death. Two individuals, both seventy-five, may nonetheless differ importantly in psychological terms because of the proximity of death in the case of one and its attendant effects.[6]

But whether there is some elusive anticipation of impending death or psychological changes near the end of life are purely psychological, there does seem to be a measure of withdrawal at a certain point.[7] And aside from caused changes, or morbid obsession, some introversion does seem called for. As long as we cannot escape death, we should prepare for it. Some might see as ideal being overtaken by death while too busy to notice its approach, but this is an unrealistic and evasive view. Impending death is too large a factor in our lives to ignore. Whatever it may bring, it affords a major opportunity for understanding and deep appreciation of the life that is about to end.

Narrative employment can be used to reconcile ourselves to impending death and so add depth to the ends of our lives. Abdicating the role of central protagonist and letting others figure more prominently in our stories is a good way to prepare for death. Reflective shaping of our narratives can help us to overcome our instinct to "go on" and to contribute to the lives of others without imposing ourselves on them. We should not deceive ourselves and strive for continuity through the memories or feelings of others. Rather we should make them more central in our narratives. In the process we will grow used to diminished roles and more readily accept the inevitability of a world without us.

Once we have some understanding of how we employ narrative to organize experience, there can be deliberate withdrawal from our central protagonist role in our own narratives and greater appreciation of the interests of others as now more important than our own. And there is compensation, for having reconciled ourselves to dying, we can take proper satisfaction in our contributions to the lives of others, not through assurances of being remembered as benefactors, but by sharing our humanity and so being part of something as long-lived as our species.

The mechanics of withdrawal from the role of central protagonist in our narratives involve suppressing our dominance and allowing other characters to grow proportionately. The key role of awareness of our use of narrative to organize experience is in opening up a distance between ourselves and our roles and so allowing deliberate diminution of those roles. Appreciation of how narrative determines who we are and how the world is allows us to take minor parts. Without that appreciation we will simply *be* characters; each given character will dominate, as it were, for our identity will be exhausted by it. When we understand that who we are at a given time is a product of such things as who we think we are and how we have structured a situation, we can distinguish ourselves from the parts we play and shape them to some extent. In this way we can lessen the coextensiveness of ourselves with particular roles. We can assume a larger, overriding perspective that encompasses those roles and allows us to manipulate them. We can then make room for the interests of others by suppressing our own and diminishing our ego predominance in our narratives. I am suggesting not that we strive for the selflessness of saints, only that we attain a measure of selflessness. Most of us have experienced diminution of self, as when a loved one eclipses us in our own stories. What is called for in old age is the same diminution, but one prompted by reflection and achieved through deliberate effort. Old age may bring some diminution of self because of absorption in the lives of children and friends, but it may also bring rigidity to our narratives because of decreased activity and parsimony. The result is that the possibility of diminution of self in a productive and healthy way is precluded by fixation on a few parsimonious stories. The point is to diminish our ego predominance knowingly and intentionally and without reducing the variety of our plots. Only in that way can we both contribute to the lives of others and benefit from our diminution. The vocabulary of narrative employment facilitates diminution by providing a way to think and speak of ourselves as characters in narratives. Once we do so, we can set about refashioning our scripts.

Conclusion: The preceding chapters outline a way of speaking and thinking of ourselves as tellers and inhabiters of stories. The proposal is something of a return to mythopoeic thinking, a partial abandonment of abstract, scientific, discursive thought, at least as it applies to certain aspects of aging. The proposal trades on the idea that as pragmatic narrators, objectivity and precision are available to us only *within* stories; the standards that determine what is objective and precise are standards we impose. The reaction will be that my proposal is a throwback and is unacceptable if only on that score. However, we are not creatures that allow for overmuch objectivity or precision, either in how we are to be understood or in how we conduct ourselves. Abstract scientific treatment of some aspects of our lives, such as aging, has a limited utility. We may productively take up the stance of the social scientist or the medical theorist and objectify aging to deal with medical and social problems. But when each of us begins to make the thousands of compromises and adjustments required by our aging bodies and the changing attitudes of others, we need more than theory. And to deal with the growing number of older people around us, we need more than theory. In both cases we need a special perspective, a way of looking at ourselves and others. This need may signal something more fundamental about the nature of knowledge, of understanding, and of the world, but we cannot wait to settle those issues prior to dealing with aging. The idiom of narrative employment can help us at two stages: first, when we must deal with human beings who are ever more distant from us as they age, and second, when we must come to terms with our own aging.

The proposal I have outlined consists of saying how we can conceptualize and describe the organization of experience in terms of storytelling and how we can then reflectively influence the lines those stories take. As for the challenges my proposal faces, they are of two different sorts. First, there are questions about the pragmatic nature of my proposal; second, there are questions about the productivity of the proposal. For the most part, the former will be rendered innocuous if the latter are answered. Philosophical and other theoretical challenges will remain, but if the proposal is taken up and proves productive, they will diminish in importance. The crux of the second sort of question is whether my proposal is cohesive and substantial enough to constitute a significantly different way of thinking and speaking. Happily, though, the latter sort of question is not one answerable by further argument. The question can be resolved only with time and practice.

Notes

Preface

1. See, e.g., James Birren, "Principles of Research on Aging", in Bernice Neugarten, ed., *Middle Age and Aging*, University of Chicago Press, 1968, pp. 547–48.
2. Malcolm Cowley, *The View From Eighty*, Penguin, 1982, p. 5.

Chapter 1

1. With respect to negative attitudes toward the elderly, see, for instance, Jack Levin and William Levin, *Ageism: Prejudice and Discrimination Against the Elderly*, Wadsworth, 1980.
2. See, e.g., a popular article on aging in *Esquire* that offers a summary of research studies: John Tierney, "The Aging Body", *Esquire*, May 1982, pp. 45–57, especially p. 52 and p. 55.
3. See, e.g., Robert N. Butler, *Why Survive? Being Old in America*, Harper & Row, 1975, especially chap. 14; John Hendrichs and C. Davis Hendrichs, *Aging in Mass Society: Myth and Realities*, Winthrop, 1981, especially pp. 159–66.
4. Ronald Blythe, *The View in Winter*, Harcourt Brace Jovanovich, 1979, p. 5.
5. See, e.g., Morton Hunt, *The Universe Within*, Simon and Schuster, 1982, pp. 285–86.

6. See George Lakoff and Mark Johnson, *Metaphors We Live By*, University of Chicago Press, 1980.

7. See Hendrichs, and Hendrichs, *Aging in Mass Society*.

8. Josef Bleicher, *Contemporary Hermeneutics*, Routledge and Kegan Paul, 1980, p. 1.

9. Richard Palmer, *Hermeneutics*, Northwestern University Press, 1969, p. 16.

Chapter 2

1. Brian Wicker, *The Story-Shaped World*, Athelone, 1975, p. 37.

2. Ibid., p. 42.

3. See Wilfrid Sellars, *Science and Metaphysics*, Routledge and Kegan Paul, 1968.

4. See Morton Hunt, *The Universe Within*, see also Jerry Fodor, *The Language of Thought*, Harvard University Press, 1975.

5. Peter Geach, *Mental Acts*, Routledge and Kegan Paul, 1957.

6. Wicker, *The Story-Shaped World*, p. 43.

7. Ibid., p. 33.

8. Gerard Genette, "The Boundaries of Narrative", *New Literary History*, vol. 8, no. 1, 1976.

9. Hayden White, "The Value of Narrativity", in W. J. T. Mitchell, ed., *On Narrative*, University of Chicago Press, 1980, pp. 1–2; my emphasis.

10. Nelson Goodman, "Twisted Tales", in Mitchell, ed., *On Narrative*, pp. 99–116.

11. Richard Rorty, "Heidegger Against the Pragmatists", mimeograph, Princeton University, 1982, p. 1. This article has not been published. Used with permission. See Rorty, *Consequences of Pragmatism*, University of Minnesota Press, 1982.

12. Rorty, "Heidegger Against the Pragmatists".

13. See, for instance, D. C. Dennett, *Content and Consciousness*, Routledge and Kegan Paul, 1969, especially chap. 3.

14. Jean Piaget, *The Language and Thought of the Child*, Routledge and Kegan Paul, 1926, pp. 15–16.

15. Ibid., pp. 19–21.

16. See, e.g., Paul Edwards, ed., *The Encyclopedia of Philosophy*, Macmillan and The Free Press, vol. 6, 1967, pp. 458–64.

17. D. M. Armstrong, "Meaning and Communication", *The Philosophical Review*, 80 (1971):427–47.

18. Howard Gardner, "The Making of a Story Teller", *Psychology Today*, March 1982, p. 49.
19. Edward S. Casey, *Imagining: A Phenomenological Study*, Indiana University Press, 1979.
20. Ibid., p. 233.
21. Ibid.
22. Gardner, "The Making of a Story Teller".
23. Rorty, "Heidegger Against the Pragmatists".
24. Ibid.

Chapter 3

1. As noted, my concern is with attitudes and perceptions, and with respect to negative attitudes and perceptions toward and of aging and the aged the following books and articles provide a fair sample:

Gordon W. Allport, *The Nature of Prejudice*, Doubleday, 1954.
F. Arnhoff and Irving Lorge, "Stereotypes about Aging and the Aged", *School and Society*, 88(1960):70–71.
Craig Aronoff, "Old Age in Prime Time", *Journal of Communications*, 24(1974):86–87.
Paul B. Baltes and K. Warner Schaie, "Aging and I.Q.: The Myth of the Twilight Years", *Psychology Today*, 7(1974):35–38, 40.
Milton L. Barron, "Minority Group Characteristics of the Aged in American Society", *Journal of Gerontology*, 8(1953):477–82.
B. D. Bell and G. G. Stanfield, "The Aging Stereotype in Experimental Perspective", *Gerontologist*, 13(1973):341–44.
Vernon L. Bengston and Neal E. Cutler, "Generations and Intergenerational Relations: Perspectives on Age Groups and Social Change", in Robert H. Binstock and Ethel Shanas, eds., *Handbook of Aging and the Social Sciences*, Van Nostrand Reinhold, 1976, pp. 130–50.
Ruth G. Bennet and J. Eckman, "Attitudes Toward Aging: A Critical Examination of Recent Literature and Implications for Future Research", in C. Eisdorfer and M. P. Lawton, eds., *The Psychology of Adult Development and Aging*, American Psychological Association, 1973, pp. 579–97.
J. H. Bunzel, "Note on the History of a Concept: Gerontophobia", *Gerontologist*, 12(1972):116–203.
Ernest W. Burgess, ed., *Aging in Western Societies*, University of Chicago Press, 1960.

Robert N. Butler, "Age-ism: Another Form of Bigotry", *Gerontologist*, 9(1969):243–46.

David J. Ciliberto, "The Influence of Perception of Old Age on Diagnosis", Master's thesis, Northeastern University, 1980.

Stephen Cutler, "Perceived Prestige Loss and Political Attitudes Among the Aged", *Gerontologist*, 13(1973):69–75.

David Hackett Fischer, *Growing Old in America*, Oxford University Press, 1977.

J. S. Francher, "It's the Pepsi Generation: Accelerated Aging and the Television Commercial", *International Journal of Aging and Human Development*, 4(1973):245–55.

Dwight Frankfather, *The Aged in the Community*, Praeger, 1977.

Edgar Z. Friedenberg, "The Generation Gap", *Annals of the American Academy of Political and Social Science*, no. 382 (1969), pp. 32–42.

Joan Hanaver, "Senior Set Unhappy With TV's Mirror", *Patriot Ledger* (Quincy, Mass.), May 13, 1976, p. 12.

Louis Harris and Associates, *The Myth and Reality of Aging in America*, National Council on Aging, 1975.

Nathan Kogan, "Attitudes Toward Old People: The Development of a Scale and an Examination of Correlates", *Journal of Abnormal and Social Psychology*, 62(1961):44–54.

Jack Levin, *The Functions of Prejudice*, Harper & Row, 1975.

Jack Levin and William C. Levin, "Perceived Age and Willingness to Interact with an Old Person", paper presented to the Annual Meeting of the Eastern Sociological Society, New York, 1977.

Jane Mills, "Attitudes of Undergraduate Students Concerning Geriatric Patients", *American Journal of Occupational Therapy*, 26(1972):200–03.

Erdman Palmore, "Attitudes Toward Aging as Shown by Humor", *Gerontologist*, 11(1971):181–86.

Erdman Palmore and F. Whittington, "Trends in the Relative Status of the Aged", *Social Forces*, 50(1971):84–9l.

Johannes T. Pedersen, "Age and Change in Public Opinion", *Public Opinion Quarterly*, 40(1976):143–53.

Charles H. Percy, *Growing Old in the Country of the Young*, McGraw-Hill, 1974.

G. R. Peters, "Self-conceptions of the Aged, Age Identification, and Aging", *Gerontologist*, 11(1971):69–73.

J. Richman, "The Foolishness and Wisdom of Age: Attitudes toward the Elderly as Reflected in Jokes", *Gerontologist*, 17(1977):210–19.

Bernard Rosen and Thomas H. Jerdee, "The Influence of Age-stereotypes on Managerial Decisions", *Journal of Applied Psychology*, 61(1976):428–32.

Phillip E. Slater, "Cultural Attitudes Toward the Aged", *Geriatrics*, 18(1963):308–14.

Mickey C. Smith, "Portrayal of the Elderly in Prescription Drug Advertising", *Gerontologist*, 16(1976):329–34.

Gordon F. Steib, "Are the Aged a Minority Group?", in Bernice Neugarten, ed., *Middle Age and Aging*, University of Chicago Press, 1965, pp. 35–46.

Claire Townsend, *Old Age: The Last Segregation*, The Center for Study of Responsive Law, Grossman, 1971.

Jacob Tuckman and Irving Lorge, "Attitudes toward Old Workers", *Journal of Applied Psychology*, 36(1952):149–53.

———. "Attitudes Toward Old People", *Journal of Social Psychology*, 37(1953):249–60.

2. See my "Armstrong and the Cybernetic Model", *Philosophy and Phenomenological Research*, 30(1970):600–602.

Chapter 4

1. Bleicher, *Contemporary Hermeneutics*, p. 22.

Chapter 5

1. On the Foster Grandparents Plan see, e.g., *Family Circle*, August 11, 1981, or contact ACTION, Foster Grandparents Program, Washington, D.C. 20525. Basically, the program, which is national in scope, employs volunteers aged sixty-five and over to work with needy children.

2. Jerry Fodor, *The Language of Thought*, Harvard University Press, 1975.

3. D. M. Armstrong, *A Materialist Theory of the Mind*, Routledge and Kegan Paul, 1968, chap. 5. See also Gilbert Ryle, *The Concept of Mind*, Hutchinson, 1949.

4. I owe the latter observation to Stephen Malikail.

5. Karl Mannheim, "Competition as a Cultural Phenomenon", quoted by Kurt Wolff, ed., *From Karl Mannheim*, Oxford University Press, 1971, p. lii.

6. John A. B. McLeish, *The Ulyssean Adult*, McGraw-Hill Ryerson, 1976, p. 4.

7. Ibid.

8. For a reflection in the analytic tradition of the notion of the anticipation of meaningfulness in the hermeneutical circle, see John Searle, *Speech Acts*, Cambridge Univeristy Press, 1969, particularly pp. 42–50. Searle, in following and criticizing H. P. Grice, considers understanding in terms of the recognition on the part of a hearer of a speaker's intention. Searle discusses that recognition in terms of sentence-meaning and the hearer's "knowledge of the rules for the sentence uttered" (p. 48). However, the notion of "uptake" on the part of a hearer seems to me to be much richer than it might appear in Searle's and consequent discussions and to be very close to that of the anticipation of meaningfulness.

Chapter 6

1. Robin Marantz Henig, *The Myth of Senility: Misconceptions About the Brain and Aging*, Doubleday, 1981.

2. Alisdair MacIntyre, "Epistemological Crises, Dramatic Narrative and the Philosophy of Science", *Monist*, 60 (1977): p. 453.

3. Ibid.

4. Ibid, p. 454.

5. Ibid.

6. Ibid, p. 455.

7. Ibid.

8. While MacIntyre's use of the idea that experience is ordered by the use of narrative is similar to my own, I do not think he would push it as far as I have tried to in conceiving of narrative employment as elemental to conceptualization. For one thing, he clearly presupposes conceptualized events that are ordered by the imposition of narratives. Moreover, I did not read MacIntyre's article until September 1983, at the prompting of a colleague, D. E. Williams. My idea of narrative employment was developed in my *Making Believe: Philosophical Reflections on Fiction* (Greenwood Press, 1984), written in 1981 and 1982. MacIntyre's *After Virtue* (Notre Dame University Press, 1981), to which I refer, also contains discussion of his narrative thesis. Again, to my loss, I did not read the book until 1983 and after having worked out my own views on narrative. It should be noted, though, that here again MacIntyre's thesis is crucially different. What he terms "narratives" I would prefer to call "histories" or narrative pat-

terns, as he is considering something fuller and less conceptually basic than I am. For one thing, he explicitly denies thinking that the narrative conception of selfhood is more basic than that of self-identity, whereas I would argue the reverse.

9. Thomas Kuhn, *The Structure of Scientific Revolution*, 2d ed., University of Chicago Press, 1970.

10. Richard Rorty, *Consequences of Pragmatism*, p. xlii.

11. The term "confused" has a technical sense in psychiatry and psychology. It is used to designate disorientation of a spatial, temporal, or contextual nature. For instance, an individual may be disoriented with respect to where he or she is, may run together events from different periods, and/or may misconstrue whether he or she is with family or strangers or is in one as opposed to another situation. A person in a nursing home may think he or she is living at home many years in the past, for example.

12. "Nursing Home Residents Savor a New Kind of Apple," *Aging*, #333/334. Nov./Dec. 1982. pp. 29–30.

13. I owe the example to Dr. Thomas Rich, of the Department of Gerontology, University of South Florida, and Dr. Mary Etten, Suncoast Geriatric Centre, Tampa, Florida, who conducted just such a workshop at the Queen's University Fourth Annual Conference on Gerontology, Kingston, Ontario, November 1983, which I attended.

14. MacIntyre, *After Virtue*, p. 197.

15. Ibid., p. 201.

16. Ibid.

17. Ibid., p. 202.

18. See my "Reference and the Composite Self", *International Studies in Philosophy*, vol. 17, no. 1, 1985.

19. Rorty, *Consequences of Pragmatism*, p. 156.

Chapter 7

1. Lucretius, *De Rerum Natura*, ed. Cyril Bailey, Oxford University Press, 1947.

2. I owe the last point to Jerome E. Bickenbach.

3. I owe my thanks to Janice Porteous for her help and comments on the wording of several of the above passages.

4. James E. Birren and K. Warner Schaie, *Handbook of the Psychology of Aging*, Van Nostrand Reinhold, 1977, p. 636, also pp. 637–42. See also Neugarten, *Middle Age and Aging*, part 9.

5. Robert Butler, "The Life Review", in Neugarten, *Middle Age and Aging*, p. 486.

6. Morton A. Lieberman, "Psychological Correlates of Impending Death", in Neugarten, *Middle Age and Aging*, pp. 509–19.

7. Ibid.

Bibliography

The following are titles referred to in the text or listed because of relevance to attitudes toward aging and the aged. Items noted or alluded to in the text are marked with an asterisk.

The literature on aging and the aged is very extensive and no bibliography can hope to be exhaustive, but I hope that the works listed here will prove useful. Generally, most of the works listed, but not referred to, support broad contentions made in the text both about attitudes toward the aged and aging and about the deteriorative aspects of aging. The latter is the reason for listing some works dealing with the biological and medical aspects of aging. The titles are sufficiently suggestive of content that I have not attempted to organize them under headings, which might prove more hindrance than help.

The reader should consult two important periodic reference works: *Areco's Quarterly Index to Periodical Literature on Aging*, published since 1981, and *Current Literature on Aging*, published quarterly by the National Council on Aging, Inc. (includes articles and abstracts). Another useful reference work is *Aging and the Aged: An Annotated Bibliography and Library Research Guide*, by L. F. Place, L. Parker, and F. J. Berghorn, published by Westview Press, 1981.

Agate, John, and Meacher, Michael, *The Care of the Old*, Fabian Society, 1969.

Allport, Gordon W., *The Nature of Prejudice*, Doubleday, 1954.

*Armstrong, D. M., *A Materialist Theory of the Mind*, Routledge and Kegan, 1968.

*————, "Meaning and Communication", *Philosophical Review* 80(1971):427–47.

Arnhoff, F., and Lorge, Irving, "Stereotypes About Aging and the Aged", *School and Society*, 88(1960):70–71.

Aronoff, Craig, "Old Age in Prime Time", *Journal of Communications*, 24(1974):86–87.

Atchley, Robert C., "The Life Course, Age Grading, and Age-linked Demands for Decision Making", in Datan, Nancy, and Ginsberg, Leon, eds., *Lifespan Development Psychology: Normative Life Crises*, Academic Press, 1975, pp. 261–78.

————, *The Social Forces in Later Life*, Wadsworth, 1977.

Baltes, Paul, *Life-span Development Psychology: Personality and Socialization*, Academic Press, 1973.

————, and Schaie, K. Warner, "Aging and I.Q.: The Myth of the Twilight Years", *Psychology Today*, 7(1974):35–38, 40.

Barron, Milton L., "Minority Group Characteristics of the Aged in American Society", *Journal of Gerontology*, 8(1953):477–82.

Barrow, G. M., "Physician's Attitude Toward Aging and the Aging Process", Ph.D dissertation, Washington University, 1971.

————, and Smith, P. A., *Aging, the Individual, and Society*, West Publishing Co., 1983.

Beeson, M. F., "Intelligence at Senescence", *Journal of Applied Psychology*, 4(1920):219–34.

Bell, B. D., and Stanfield, G. G., "The Aging Stereotype in Experimental Perspective", *Gerontologist*, 13(1973):341–44.

Bell, Tony, "The Relationship Between Social Involvement and Feeling Old Among Residents in Homes for the Aged", *Journal of Gerontology*, 22(1967):17–22.

Bengston, Vernon L., and Cutler, Neal E., "Generations and Intergenerational Relations: Perspectives on Age Groups and Social Change", in Binstock, Robert H., and Shanas, Ethel, eds., *Handbook of Aging and the Social Sciences*, Van Nostrand Reinhold, 1976.

Bennet, J. C., *The Ethics of Aging: Church Mission and Practice*, Pittsburgh Theological Seminary, 1982.

Bennet, Ruth G., and Eckman, J., "Attitudes Toward Aging: A Critical Examination of Recent Literature and Implications for Future Research", in Eisdorfer, C., and Lawton, M. P., eds., *The Psychology of Adult Development and Aging*, American Psychological Association, 1973, pp. 579–97.

Berghorn, F. J., and Place, L. F., "Aging Now and in the Future: A Social Perspective", *Journal of Social Welfare*, 5(1978):33–40.

————, and Schafer, D. E., *The Dynamics of Aging: Original Essays on the Processes and Experiences of Growing Old*, Westview Press, 1981.

Bierman, E., and Hazzard, W., "Biology of Aging", in Smith, D. W.; Bierman, E. L.; and Robinson, N. M., eds., *The Biologic Ages of Man from Conception Through Old Age*, W. B. Saunders, 1978.

Binstock, R. H., "Interest-group Liberalism and the Politics of Aging", *Gerontologist*, 12(1972):265–80.

————, and Shanas, Ethel, eds., *Handbook of Aging and the Social Sciences*, Van Nostrand Reinhold, 1976.

Birren, James, ed., *Handbook of Aging and the Individual*, University of Chicago Press, 1959.

————, "Aging: Psychological Aspects", in Sills, David, ed., *The International Encyclopedia of the Social Sciences*, vol. 1, Macmillan, 1968.

————, "Psychological Aspects of Aging: Intellectual Functioning", *Gerontologist*, 8(1968):16–19.

*————, "Principles of Research on Aging", in Neugarten, Bernice, ed., *Middle Age and Aging*, University of Chicago Press, 1968, pp. 547–48.

————. "Progress in Research on Aging in the Behavioural and Social Sciences", *Human Development*, 23(1980):33–45.

————, and Schaie, K. Warner, eds., *Handbook of the Psychology of Aging*, Van Nostrand Reinhold, 1977.

————, and Sloane, R. B., eds., *Handbook of Mental Health and Aging*, Springer, 1980.

Blau, Zena, "Structural Constraints on Friendships in Old Age", *American Sociological Review*, 26(1961):429–39.

————. *Old Age in a Changing Society*, New Viewpoints, 1973.

*Bleicher, Josef, *Contemporary Hermeneutics*, Routledge and Kegan Paul, 1980.

Blythe, Ronald, *The View in Winter*, Harcourt Brace Jovanovich, 1979.

Bock, E. Wilbur, "Aging and Suicide: The Significance of Marital, Kinship, and Alternative Relations", *Family Coordinator*, 21(1972):71–80.

Bogomolets, A. A., *The Prolongation of Life*, Duell, Sloan and Pearce, 1946.

Botwinick, Jack, *Cognitive Processes in Maturity and Old Age*, Springer, 1967.

————. *Aging and Behaviour*, Springer, 1973.

Boucheron, Pierre, *How to Enjoy Life After Sixty*, Archer House, 1959.

Brandt-Ryan, Barbara, "Attitudes Toward and Responses to Aging", Ph.D dissertation, University of Colorado, 1978.

Breen, Leonard, "The Aging Individual", in Tibbits, Clark, ed., *Handbook of Social Gerontology*, University of Chicago Press, 1960.

Bromley, D. B., *The Psychology of Human Aging*, Penguin, 1974.

Brown, R. N., *Rights of Older Persons: The Basic A.C.L.U. Guide to an Older Person's Rights*, Avon Books, 1979.

Bunzel, J. H., "Note on the History of a Concept: Gerontophobia", *Gerontologist*, 12(1972):116–23.

Burgess, Ernest W., ed., *Aging in Western Societies*, University of Chicago Press, 1960.

*Butler, Robert, "The Life Review", in Neugarten, Bernice, ed., *Middle Age and Aging*, University of Chicago Press, 1968, pp. 486–96.

———, "Age-ism: Another Form of Bigotry", *Gerontologist*, 9(1969): 243–46.

*———, *Why Survive? Being Old in America*, Harper & Row, 1975.

———, and Lewis, M. I., *Aging and Mental Health*, C. V. Mosby, 1973.

Cain, Leonard, "Aging and the Law", in Binstock, Robert, and Shanas, Ethel, eds., *Handbook of Aging and the Social Sciences*, Van Nostrand Reinhold, 1976, pp. 342–63.

Cape, R. D. T., "The Aging Human", in Singhal, S. K., Sinclair, N. R., and Stiller, C. R., eds., *Aging and Immunity*, Elsevier/North Holland, 1979, pp. 213–23.

*Casey, Edward S., *Imagining: A Phenomenological Study*, Indiana University Press, 1979.

Cassel, C., and Jameton, A. L., "Dementia in the Elderly: An Analysis of Medical Responsibility", *Annals of Internal Medicine*, 94(1981):802–07.

Cavan, Ruth, "Self and Role in Adjustment During Old Age", in Rose, Arnold, ed., *Human Behaviour and Social Processes*, Houghton-Mifflin, 1962, pp. 526–36.

Chappell, N. L., "Informal Support Networks Among the Elderly", *Research on Aging*, 5(1983):77–79.

Chatfield, W. F., "Economic and Sociological Factors Influencing Life Satisfaction of the Aged", *Journal of Gerontology*, 32(1977):593–99.

Chown, Sheila, *Human Ageing*, Penguin, 1972.

Christiansen, D., "Dignity in Aging", *The Hastings Center Report*, 4 (1974):6–8.

Ciliberto, David J., "The Influence of Perception of Old Age on Diagnosis", Master's thesis, Northeastern University, 1980.

Clark, M., and Anderson, B., *Culture and Aging*, Charles C. Thomas, 1967.

Cole, T. R., "The 'Enlightened' View of Aging: Victorian Morality in a New Key", *Hasting Center Report*, 13(1983):34–40.

Comfort, Alex, *Aging: The Biology of Senescence*, Holt, Rinehart and Winston, 1964.

————, *The Process of Aging*, New American Library, 1964.

————, *Ageing*, Routledge and Kegan Paul, 1964.

Cowgill, Donald, and Holmes, Lewelyn, *Aging and Modernization*, Appleton-Century Crofts, 1972.

*Cowley, Malcolm, *The View From Eighty*, Penguin, 1982.

Craik, F. I. M., "Age Differences in Human Memory", in Birren, James, and Schaie, K. Warner, eds., *Handbook of the Psychology of Aging*, Van Nostrand Reinhold, 1977, pp. 384–420.

Cryns, A. G., and Monk, A., "Attitudes of the Aged Toward the Young: A Multivariate Study of Intergenerational Perception", *Journal of Gerontology*, 27(1972):107–12.

————, "Attitudes Toward Youth as a Function of Adult Age: A Multivariate Study of Intergenerational Dynamics", *International Journal of Aging and Human Development*, 4(1973):23–33.

Curtin, Sharon, *Nobody Ever Died of Old Age*, Little, Brown, 1972.

Cutler, Stephen, "Perceived Prestige Loss and Political Attitudes Among the Aged", *Gerontologist*, 13(1973):69–75.

Davis, J. F., *Minority-Dominant Relations*, AHM Publishing, 1978.

de Beauvoir, Simone, *The Coming of Age*, Putnam's Sons, 1972.

*Dennett, D. C., *Content and Consciousness*, Routledge and Kegan Paul, 1969.

Denny, N. W., "Problems Solving in Later Adulthood", in Baltes, P. B., and Brimm, O. G., eds., *Life-span Development and Behaviour*, vol. 2, Academic Press, 1979, pp. 37–66.

Drevenstedt, Jean, "Perceptions of Onset of Young Adulthood, Middle Age, and Old Age", *Journal of Gerontology*, 31(1976):53–57.

Ebersole, P., and Hess, P., *Toward Healthy Aging: Human Needs and the Nursing Response*, C.V. Mosby, 1981.

Edwards, Paul, ed., *The Encyclopedia of Philosophy*, Macmillan and The Free Press, 1967.

Eisdorfer, C., and Lawton, M. P., eds., *The Psychology of Adult Development and Aging*, American Psychological Association, 1973.

Elder, G., *The Alienated: Growing Old Today*, Writers and Readers Co-op, 1979.

Finch, C. E., and Hayflick, L., eds., *Handbook of the Biology of Aging*, Van Nostrand Reinhold, 1977.

Fischer, David Hackett, *Growing Old in America*, Oxford University Press, 1977.

*Fodor, Jerry, *The Language of Thought*, Harvard University Press, 1975.

Foster, J. C., and Taylor, G. A., "The Applicability of Mental Tests to Persons over Fifty Years of Age", *Journal of Applied Psychology*, 4(1920):39–58.

Francher, J. S., "It's the Pepsi Generation: Accelerated Aging and the Television Commercial", *International Journal of Aging and Human Development*, 4(1973):245–55.

Frankfather, Dwight, *The Aged in the Community*, Praeger, 1977.

Friedenberg, Edgar Z., "The Generation Gap", *Annals of the American Academy of Political and Social Science*, 382(1969):32–42.

Gadow, S., "Medicine, Ethics and the Elderly", *Gerontologist*, 20(1980):680–85.

*Gardner, Howard, "The Making of a Story Teller", *Psychology Today*, March 1982.

Garvin, Richard, and Burger, Robert, *Where They Go To Die: The Tragedy of America's Aged*, Delacorte Press, 1968.

*Geach, Peter, *Mental Acts*, Routledge and Kegan Paul, 1957.

*Genette, Gerard, "The Boundaries of Narrative", *New Literary History*, vol 8, no. 1, 1976.

Glenn, Norval, "Aging, Disengagement, and Opinionation", *Public Opinion Quarterly*, 33(1969):17–33.

Gold, Byron; Kutza, Elizabeth; and Marmor, Theodore, "United States Social Policy on Old Age: Present Patterns and Predictions", in Neugarten, Bernice, and Havighurst, Robert, eds., *Social Policy, Social Ethics, and the Aging Society*, U.S. Goverment Printing Office, 1976, pp. 9–22.

Golde, P., and Kogan, N. A., "A Sentence Completion Procedure for Assessing Attitudes Toward Old People", *Journal of Gerontology*, 14(1959):355–63.

Goldman, R., "Decline in Organ Function With Aging", in Rossman, I., ed., *Clinical Geriatrics*, J. B. Lippincott, 1979, pp. 23–59.

Goode, William, *The Family*, Prentice-Hall, 1964.

*Goodman, Nelson, "Twisted Tales", in W. J. T. Mitchell, ed., *On Narrative*, University of Chicago Press, 1980. pp. 99–116.

Gordon, T. J., "Prospects for Aging in America", in Riley, M. W., ed., *Aging from Birth to Death: Interdisciplinary Perspectives*, Westview Press, 1979, pp. 179–96.

Gray, Robert, and Kasteler, Josephine, "An Evaluation of a Foster Grandparent Project", *Sociology and Social Research*, 54(1970):181–89.

Gross, R.; Gross, B.; and Seidman, S., eds., *The New Old: Struggling for Decent Aging*, Anchor Press, 1978.

Hall, G. Stanley, *Senescence: The Last Half of Life*, Appleton, 1923.

Hanaver, Joan, "Senior Set Unhappy with TV's Mirror", *Patriot Ledger*, May 13, 1976.

Hareven, T. K., and Adams, K. J., eds., *Aging and Life Course Transitions: An Interdisciplinary Perspective*, Guilford, 1982.

Harris, Louis, and associates, *The Myth and Reality of Aging in America*, National Council on Aging, 1975.

Hastings Center Study Group, *Treatment of Elderly Patients With Impaired or Diminished Competency*, Hastings Center, 1984.

Haug, M. R., ed., *Elderly Patients and Their Doctors*, Springer, 1981.

Havighurst, Robert, "Successful Aging", in Williams, Richard; Tibbits, Clark; and Donahue, William, eds., *Processes of Aging*, vol. 1, Atherton, 1963, pp. 229–320.

———, "Personality and Patterns of Aging", *Gerontologist*, 8(1968):20–23.

———, "A Social-psychological Perspective on Aging", *Gerontologist*, 8(1968):67–71.

*Hendrichs, John, and Hendrichs, C. Davis, *Aging in Mass Society: Myth and Realities*, Winthrop, 1981.

*Henig, Robin Marantz, *The Myth of Senility: Misconceptions About the Brain and Aging*, Doubleday, 1981.

Heron, Alastair, and Chown, Sheila, *Age and Function*, Little, Brown, 1967.

Hickey, Tom; Hickey, Louise; and Kalish, Richard, "Children's Perceptions of the Elderly", *Journal of Genetic Psychology*, 112(1968):227–35.

Hinchcliffe, B., "Aging and Sensory Thresholds", *Journal of Gerontology* 17(1962):45–50.

Hinton, John, *Dying*, Penguin, 1972.

Hite, Shere, *The Hite Report*, Dell, 1976.

Hochschild, A. R., "Communal Life Styles for the Old", *Society*, 10(1973):50–57.

Hoffmeister, F., and Muller, C., eds., *Brain Function in Old Age: Evaluation of Change and Disorders*, Springer, 1979.

Holzberg, C. S., "Ethnicity and Aging: Anthropological Perspectives on More Than the Minority Elderly", *Gerontologist*, 22(1982):137–42.

Howell, C. I., "Old Age", *Geriatrics*, 4(1949):281–92.

———, "Senile Deterioration of the Central Nervous System", *British Medical Journal*, 1(1949):56–58.

*Hunt, Morton, *The Universe Within*, Simon and Schuster, 1982.

Jacobs, Jerry, *Fun City: An Ethnographic Study of a Retirement Community*, Holt, Rinehart and Winston, 1974.

Jarvik, Lissy, *Psychological Symptoms and Cognitive Loss in the Elderly*, Halsted, 1979.

Jerome, Edward, "Age and Learning-experimental Studies", in Birren, James, ed., *Handbook of Aging and the Individual*, University of Chicago Press, 1959, pp. 655–99.

Jones, Harold, "Intelligence and Problem-solving", in Birren, James, ed., *Handbook of Aging and the Individual*, University of Chicago Press, 1959. pp. 700–38.

Jones, Rochelle, *The Other Generation: The New Power of Older People*, Prentice-Hall, 1977.

Kahana, Eva; Liang, Jersey; Felton, Barbara; Fairchild, Thomas; and Harel, Zev, "Perspectives of Aged on Victimization, 'Ageism', and Their Problems in Urban Society", *Gerontologist*, 17(1977):121–29.

Kalish, R. A., *Late Adulthood: Perspectives on Human Development*, Brooks/Cole, 1975.

———, "The New Ageism and the Failure Models: A Polemic", *Gerontologist*, 19(1979):398–402.

Kleinberg, S. J., "The Role of the Humanities in Gerontological Research", *Gerontologist*, 18(1978):574–76.

Kogan, Nathan, "Attitudes Toward Old People: The Development of a Scale and an Examination of Correlates", *Journal of Abnormal and Social Psychology*, 62(1961):44–54.

Koller, Marvin, *Social Gerontology*, Random House, 1968.

Kuhlen, Raymond, "Age and Intelligence: The Significance of Cultural Change in Longitudinal versus Cross-sectional Findings", in Neugarten, Bernice, ed., *Middle Age and Aging*, University of Chicago Press, 1968, pp. 552–62.

*Kuhn, Thomas, *The Structure of Scientific Revolution*, 2d ed., University of Chicago Press, 1970.

*Lakoff, George, and Johnson, Mark, *Metaphors We Live By*, University of Chicago Press, 1980.

Lehman, H., *Age and Achievement*, Princeton University Press, 1953.

Levin, Jack, *The Functions of Prejudice*, Harper & Row, 1975.

*———, and Levin, William C., "Perceived Age and Willingness to Interact with an Older Person", paper presented to the Annual Meeting of the Eastern Sociological Society, New York, 1977.

*———, *Ageism: Prejudice and Discrimination Against the Elderly*, Wadsworth, 1980.

*Lieberman, Morton A., "Psychological Correlates of Impending Death", in Neugarten, Bernice, ed., *Middle Age and Aging*, University of Chicago Press, 1968, pp. 509–19.

Lobsenz, Norman, "Sex and the Senior Citizen", *New York Times Magazine,* January 20, 1974.

Long, Barbara; Ziller, Robert; and Thompson, Elaine, "A Comparison of Prejudices: the Effects Upon Friendship Ratings of Chronic Illness, Old Age, Education, and Race", *Journal of Social Psychology,* 70(1960):101–9.

*Lucretius, *De Rerum Natura,* ed. Cyril Bailey, Oxford University Press, 1947.

Maas, H. S., *People and Contexts: Social Development from Birth to Old Age,* Prentice-Hall, 1984.

*MacIntyre, Alisdair, "Epistemological Crises, Dramatic Narrative and the Philosophy of Science", *Monist,* 60, (1977) pp. 453–72.

*———, *After Virtue,* Notre Dame University Press, 1981.

McKee, P. L., ed., *Philosophical Foundations of Gerontology,* Human Sciences Press, 1981.

*McLeish, John A. B., *The Ulyssean Adult,* McGraw-Hill Ryerson, 1976.

McPherson, B. D., *Aging and the Social Process,* Butterworth, 1983.

McTavish, Donald, "Perceptions of Old People: A Review of Research, Methodologies, and Findings", *Gerontologist,* 11(1971):90–101.

Manaster, Al, "Therapy with the 'Senile' Geriatric Patient", *International Journal of Group Psychology,* 22(1972):250–57.

*Mannheim, Karl "Competition as a Cultural Phenomenon", quoted by Kurt Wolff, ed., *From Karl Mannheim,* Oxford University Press, 1971.

Meacher, Michael, *Taken for a Ride: Special Residential Homes for Confused Old People,* Longman Group, 1972.

Miles, Catherine, "The Influence of Speed and Age on Intelligence Scores of Adults", *Journal of Genetic Psychology,* 10(1934):208–10.

Miller, Stephen, "The Social Dilemma of the Aging Leisure Participant", in Rose, Arnold, and Peterson, Warren, eds., *Older People and Their Social World,* F. A. Davis, 1965.

Mills, Jane, "Attitudes of Undergraduate Students Concerning Geriatric Patients", *American Journal of Occupational Therapy,* 26(1972):200–03.

*Mitchell, W. J. T., ed. *On Narrative,* University of Chicago Press, 1980.

Neugarten, Bernice, "The Old and Young in Modern Societies", *American Behavioural Scientist,* 14(1970):13–24.

———, "Personality and the Aging Process", in Zarit, Steven, ed., *Readings in Aging and Death: Contemporary Perspectives,* Harper & Row, 1977.

*————, ed., *Middle Age and Aging*, University of Chicago Press, 1968.

————, and associates, *Personality in Middle and Later Life*, Atherton Press, 1964.

————, and Hall, E., "Acting One's Age: New Rules for Old", *Psychology Today*, 13(1980):66.

*Palmer, Richard, *Hermeneutics*, Northwestern University Press, 1969.

Palmore, Erdman, "Sociological Aspects of Aging", in Busse, E. W., and Pfeiffer, E., eds., *Behaviour and Adaptation in Later Life*, Little, Brown, 1969, pp. 33–69.

————, "The Effects of Aging on Activities and Attitudes", in Palmore, Erdman, ed., Normal Aging, Duke University Press, 1970, pp. 332–41.

*————, "Attitudes Toward Aging as Shown by Humor", *Gerontologist*, 11(1971):181–86.

————, *Social Patterns in Normal Aging: Findings from the Duke Longitudinal Study*, Duke University Press, 1981.

————, ed., *Normal Aging*, Duke University Press, 1981.

————, ed., *International Handbook on Aging: Contemporary Developments and Research*, Greenwood Press, 1980.

————, and Whittington, F., "Trends in the Relative Status of the Aged", *Social Forces*, 50(1971):84–91.

Parsons, Talcott, "Toward a Healthy Maturity", *Journal of Health and Human Behaviour*, 1(1960):163–73.

Pedersen, Johannes T., "Age and Change in Public Opinion", *Public Opinion Quarterly*, 40(1976):143–53.

Percy, Charles H., *Growing Old in the Country of the Young*,, McGraw-Hill, 1974.

Peters, G. R., "Self-conceptions of the Aged, Age Identification, and Aging", *Gerontologist*, 11(1971):69–73.

Phillips, Bernard, "A Role Theory Approach to Adjustment in Old Age", *American Sociological Review*, 22(1957):212–17.

————, "Role Change, Subjective Age and Adjustment: A Correlational Analysis", *Journal of Gerontology*, 16(1961):347–52.

*Piaget, Jean, *The Language and Thought of the Child*, Routledge and Kegan Paul, 1926.

*Prado, C. G., "Reference and the Composite Self ", *International Studies in Philosophy*, vol. 17, no. 1, 1985.

*————, *Making Believe: Philosophical Reflections on Fiction*, Greenwood Press, 1984.

*————, "Armstrong and the Cybernetic Model", *Philosophy and Phenomenological Research*, 30(1970):600–602.

Rabushka, A., and Jacobs, B., *Old Folks at Home*, The Free Press, 1980.

Ratzan, R. M., "Being Old Makes You Different", *The Hastings Center Report*, 10(1980):32–42.

Reichard, Suzanne; Livson, Florine; and Petersen, Paul, *Aging and Personality*, John Wiley, 1962.

Richman, J., "The Foolishness and Wisdom of Age: Attitudes toward the Elderly as Reflected in Jokes", *Gerontologist*, 17(1977):210–19.

Riley, Matilda, "Social Gerontology and the Age Stratification of Society", *Gerontologist*, 11(1971):79–87.

——, "Age Strata in Social Systems", in Binstock, Robert, and Shanas, Ethel, eds., *Handbook of Aging and the Social Sciences*, Van Nostrand Reinhold, 1976, pp. 189–217.

——, "Aging, Social Change, and the Power of Ideas", *Daedelus*, 107(1978):39–52.

——, and Foner, Anne, *Aging and Society, vol. 1, An Inventory of Research Findings*, Russell Sage Foundation, 1968.

——; Riley, John; and Johnston, Marilyn, *Aging and Society, vol. 2, Aging and the Professions*, Russell Sage Foundation, 1969.

*Rorty, Richard, "Heidegger Against the Pragmatists", mimeograph, Princeton University, 1982, p. 1. This article has not been published. Used with permission.

*——, *Consequences of Pragmatism*, University of Minnesota Press, 1982.

*——, *Philosophy and the Mirror of Nature*, Princeton University Press, 1979.

Rose, Arnold, "Physical Health and Mental Outlook Among the Aging", in Rose, Arnold, and Peterson, Warren, eds., *Older People and Their Social World*, F. A. Davis, 1965, pp. 210–69.

Rosen, Bernard, and Jerdee, Thomas H., "The Influence of Age-stereotypes on Managerial Decisions", *Journal of Applied Psychology*, 61(1976):428–32.

*Ryle, Gilbert, *The Concept of Mind*, Hutchinson, 1949.

Schulz, J. H., *The Economics of Aging*, Wadsworth, 1976.

*Searle, John, *Speech Acts*, Cambridge University Press, 1969.

Seefeldt, Carol; Jantz, Richard; Galpher, Alice; and Serock, Kathy, "Using Pictures to Explore Children's Attitudes toward the Elderly", *Gerontologist*, 17(1977):506–12.

Seeman, Melvin, "Intellectual Perspective and Adjustment to Minority Status", *Social Problems*, 3(1956):142–53.

*Sellars, Wilfrid, *Science and Metaphysics*, Routledge and Kegan Paul, 1968.

Shanas, Ethel, *The Health of Older People: A Social Survey*, Harvard University Press, 1962.

Siegler, Ilene, "Aging IQs," *Human Behavior*, 5(1976):55.

Simpson, G. A., *A Study of Middle Age Persons' Concept of Their Own Early Old Age*, Catholic University of America, 1979.

Slater, Phillip E., "Cultural Attitudes Toward the Aged", *Geriatrics*, 18(1963):308–14.

Smith, Mickey C., "Portrayal of the Elderly in Prescription Drug Advertising", *Gerontologist*, 16(1976):329–34.

Spiker, S. F.; Woodward, K. M.; and Van Tassel, D. D., eds., *Aging and the Elderly: Humanistic Perspectives in Gerontology*, Humanities Press, 1978.

Strehler, Bernard, *Time, Cells, and Aging,,* Academic Press, 1962.

Streib, Gordon F., "Are the Aged a Minority Group?", in Neugarten, Bernice, ed., *Middle Age and Aging*, University of Chicago Press, 1965, pp. 35–46.

———, "Social Stratification and Aging", in Binstock, Robert, and Shanas, Ethel, eds., *Handbook of Aging and the Social Sciences*, Van Nostrand Reinhold, 1976, pp. 160–88.

———, and Thompson, Wayne, "The Older Person in a Family Context", in Tibbets, Clark, ed., *Handbook of Social Gerontology*, University of Chicago Press, 1960, pp. 447–88.

*Tierney, John, "The Aging Body", *Esquire*, May 1982, pp. 45–57.

Townsend, Claire, *Old Age: The Last Segregation*, The Center for Study of Responsive Law, Grossman, 1971.

Tuckman, Jacob, and Lorge, Irving, "Attitudes toward Old Workers", *Journal of Applied Psychology*, 36(1952):149–53.

———, "Attitudes Toward Older People", *Journal of Social Psychology*, 37:(1953):249–60.

———, "Classification of the Self as Young, Middle-aged, or Old", *Geriatrics*, 9(1954):534–36.

Vischer, Adolph Lucas, *On Growing Old*, trans. Onn, Gerald, Allen and Unwin, 1966.

*White, Hayden, "The Value of Narrativity", in W. J. T. Mitchell, ed., *On Narrative*, University of Chicago Press, 1980, pp. 1–23.

*Wicker, Brian, *The Story-Shaped World*, Athelone, 1975.

Winiecke, Linda, "The Appeal of Age Segregated Housing to the Elderly Poor", *International Journal of Aging and Human Development*, 4(1973):293–306.

Wood, V., "Age-appropriate Behavior for Older People", *Gerontologist*, 11(1971):74–78.

Zinberg, Norman, and Kaufman, Irving, *Normal Psychology of the Aging*, International Universities Press, 1963.

Zola, I. K., "Feeling about Age Among Older People", *Journal of Gerontology*, 17(1962):65–68.

Index

About the Author

C. G. PRADO is Professor of Philosophy and the Departmental Chairman of Graduate Studies at Queen's University in Kingston, Ontario. He is the author of *Making Believe: Philosophical Reflections on Fiction* (Greenwood Press, 1984) and *Illusions of Faith: A Critique of Noncredal Religion,* as well as numerous articles in philosophical journals.